Do You Want to
Make Money or
Would You Rather
Fool Around?

BOOKS BY JOHN SPOONER

The Foursome

Sex and Money

Smart People

The King of Terrors

Class (by *Brutus*)

Confessions of a Stockbroker
(by *Brutus*)

Three Cheers for War in General

The Pheasant-Lined Vest
of Charlie Freeman

Do You Want to
Make Money or
Would You Rather
Fool Around?

John D. Spooner

Adams Media Corporation
Holbrook, Massachusetts

Published by
Adams Media Corporation
260 Center Street, Holbrook, MA 02343

ISBN: 1-58062-245-3

Printed in the United States of America.

J I H G F E D C B A

Library of Congress Cataloging-in-Publication Data
Spooner, John D.
Do you want to make money or would you rather fool around? /
by John D. Spooner.
p.   cm.
ISBN 1-58062-245-3
1. Investments. 2. Finance, Personal. I. Title.
HG4521.S718   1999
332.6—dc21   99-33983
CIP

This publication is designed to provide accurate and authoritative information with regard to the subject matter covered. It is sold with the understanding that the publisher is not engaged in rendering legal, accounting,
or other professional advice. If legal advice or other expert assistance is
required, the services of a competent professional person should be sought.
—From a *Declaration of Principles* jointly adopted by
a Committee of the American Bar Association and
a Committee of Publishers and Associations

This book is available at quantity discounts for bulk purchases.
For information, call 1-800-872-5627.

Visit our home page at http://www.businesstown.com

Dedication

For my crew in Spooner's Alley, who give me and our clients extraordinary value added every day: my son Scott, Bridget, Yvonne, Lauri and Courtney.

Acknowledgments

Countless people have helped me on my journey to completing this book. But I must single out a few of the most special whose insights, guidance and senses of humor kept me on track: my agent Ike Williams, my editor Edward Walters, my editorial assistant Yvonne Russell, my special spies William Boyce and Bill Eisen, and Robert Smith, and as always, my good conscience and wife, Susan.

Author's Note

By the time you read this book, the stock prices of many of the companies mentioned will, obviously, have changed. Some stocks may also have split, or raised their dividends.

While this book is full of colorful stories and, I hope, some useful and profitable advice, I cannot advise you on your specific situation. I don't know you as well as I know the people in this book—I don't know your goals, your resources, or your tolerance for risk.

What I do know is that as an investor, you'll experience ups and downs as dramatic as those in any soap opera—hopefully, the lessons in these stories can help you avoid the tragic consequences that can afflict the characters in TV's daytime series.

If you're serious about making money, though, there is no substitute for doing your own research, making your own decisions, and getting professional investment counseling if you need it. This book does not purport to provide any investment counseling or other professional service.

The characters in this book, except for my family, are in most cases fictitious. While the situations are derived from my own experience (and the opinions entirely my own), each one has been deliberately altered to confound, confuse, and otherwise render identification of the principals impossible.

Still, fear and greed reign eternal. Only the buzzwords differ, from market cycle to market cycle, from fad to fad. The lessons discussed in these stories about the way people deal with their money will be as true at the next millenium as they are today.

— JOHN D. SPOONER

Contents

MARKET STRATEGIES

RESEARCH AND DEVELOPMENT

WHOM CAN YOU TRUST?

IT'S YOUR MONEY

LESSONS FROM HISTORY

PEOPLE AND MONEY

Introduction

I GREW UP IN THE INVESTMENT BUSINESS. My father was a partner in an old New York firm that had branches all over the United States and in Europe. He was a very old-fashioned man, courtly and reserved. He preached the importance of understanding and studying history—as well as common sense. "Always marry funny," was one of his pieces of advice to me, when most fathers seemed to counsel, "Marry money." While in school, I worked part time in his office doing odd jobs and listening to the brokers and the clients spouting both wisdom and foolishness.

When it comes to money, I have seen it all. I was trading stocks when John F. Kennedy was assassinated; when you couldn't give a stock away in the 1970s; when Nixon negotiated with China, and then was forced to resign because of Watergate; when there were gas lines and 20 percent inflation; when the market crashed in 1987 in the biggest one-day decline in history.

I currently watch more than half a billion dollars for clients all over the world, from Hong Kong to Santa Barbara, from London to Houston, from Israel to Pacific Palisades. My clients range from heads of foundations to the CEOs of multibillion-dollar corporations, the chairmen of Big Eight accounting firms, international architects, mystery novelists, news anchors, sports commentators, Pulitzer Prize winners, movie producers, bank presidents, wine merchants, eastern European entrepreneurs, venture capitalists, and so many more. They represent an incredible plum pudding of fascinating characters—and they educate me daily.

I'd like to pass the wisdom of this experience on to you. The lessons I've learned have held in good markets and bad, through wars, recessions, crashes, and booms. They've stood the test of time—and they should help you, whether you are a bull or a bear, a buyer or a seller.

I have a needlepoint pillow given to me by a client on which is written, "You never know anyone until you deal with their money." This is true. This is an extremely personal business. It brings out the best—and the worst—in people. It involves planning and knowledge of not only your clients' net worth, but also of their children and parents, their hobbies, their secrets, their dreams for the future.

I keep a cartoon that a client sent me years ago posted on my office bulletin board. It shows a patient lying on a psychiatrist's couch. The shrink sits in a chair next to the patient and says, "Shudda, wudda, cudda ... Next!" Along with it, my client sent this note: "This is what you do." Investing is a psychiatric profession; it deals much more with emotion than with balance sheets and income statements.

You may not have heard advice like this from an investment "expert" before. My approach is more about the head and the heart of the investor than about the nuts and bolts of investing. But I think these lessons will serve you well as you try to make smart choices about your own money.

MARKET

STRATEGIES

Do You Really Want to Make Money?

I N THE EARLY 1960S, I WAS BEING TRAINED ON Wall Street to be a stockbroker. Only Merrill Lynch had a formal training program in those days; everyone else seemed to believe in on-the-job training. Boardrooms were where all the brokers sat surrounded by customers, many of whom were regulars. The customers spent part of every day watching the ticker tape parade go by on the wall, trading stocks and stories. Brokerage offices were like social clubs then. Broker and client knew each other. Often a stockbroker was a family counselor and friend. The clients would come into the boardrooms as they would a neighborhood bar like Cheers: a place to be social, a place to keep warm, a place where everybody knew your name.

Big Arthur was a boardroom regular, a shoe dog by trade, a salesman of ladies' shoes. Whenever he was not on the road for his company, he sat in a front row seat, a row reserved for customers. And he traded stocks. Every day that he saw me, he would say the same thing. "Don't get old," he would say, "whatever you do, don't get old." Then he'd pat an empty seat next to him. "Sit with me, kid. What good is life if you can't lie to the next generation?" Big Arthur wore English-cut suits and highly polished shoes. "Dress British, think Yiddish," he told me. "Contrast is everything in life. I act different than I dress, so it always surprises people. If you surprise people, they usually like having you around." He would go on. "When my father came here from a little village outside of Krakow, Poland, he told me to 'lose the ghetto,' become American. This is what I tried to do, and he also told me never to lose the Kop. The head! But he would never stay in a stock for more than two weeks. He'd make a few bucks, lose a few bucks."

"You can never really make any money that way," I pointed out to him after I had known him long enough to dare a suggestion of my own.

"I've already made my money," he replied. "But let me tell you something. In my business, the shoe business, they say 'the smell of leather keeps us together.' We gamble every day on style, and price, and a million other things. There is no such thing as an easy business. Only from the outside does anything appear so. Trading the market is entertainment for me, a place to fool around, a little kibbitz, as they say."

"I could tell you about a stock that I think can double in two years," I told Big Arthur.

He looked at me and smiled. "How do I know I'm going to live that long?" Because of Arthur, I have asked every new prospective client who comes into my office, "Are you serious about making money, or do you just want to fool around?" You'd be amazed at the number of people who have to think a while before answering.

The Second Part of Every Trade

THERE ARE TWO PARTS TO EVERY SELL DECISION when you decide to get out of a stock. One part is, at what price do I exit this stock position? (Part of this is also, what are my tax implications if I sell?) The second part, and almost as important, is, what do I do with the money when I sell? Very few people pay enough attention to the second part of the equation.

I have a friend who, several years ago, bought Exxon at $40—for all the right reasons, I thought. He thought Exxon was well managed, paid a good dividend, and was well positioned to serve the growing worldwide demand for energy that he thought would kick in as countries increasingly moved toward free-market economies. After holding it for several years, the stock moved to the high $60s.

"I want to sell Exxon," my friend said. "I've got a good profit. Bulls make money; bears can make money. Pigs never make money."

"Ahhh," I told him, "the old cliché. But, you know, pigs often make more money than anyone else. Because they are not afraid to take a large position and they ride it. Warren Buffet is, essentially, a pig by this definition." Warren Buffett is the second wealthiest American after Bill Gates; Buffett made his money in the stock market.

My friend sold his Exxon at $70, paid his taxes, and within a week bought Compaq Computer at $42. "It's down from the $50s. I think it's cheap. Also," he reasoned, "I sold 1,000 Exxon and I bought 1,600 Compaq, same amount of money, one and a half the amount of stock." Exxon subsequently moved on to all-time-high prices, and it still paid a healthy dividend to boot. Compaq dropped over the half year to as low as $22. And it paid nothing.

This kind of maneuver is comparable to quitting a job before you have another one to go to. When you make a decision to sell a stock, think about the second part of the transaction: What do I do with the money after I sell? And ask yourself this question: Is what I do with the proceeds going to be half as good as holding the stock I'm selling? Most of the time it won't be.

A Simple Test for
Holding a Stock

PEOPLE MOVE PORTFOLIOS INTO MY CARE ALL the
time. These are usually mixed bags of securities, some good, some awful. When I go over the holdings and ask, "How come you own *this*?" about a specific
investment, most people say, "I have no idea," as though
a gremlin had put it in their portfolio. But more likely, it
was an old recommendation from a broker, a friend, or a
relative. And they've blocked it from their minds.

I have a simple test for the ownership of all stocks:
Can you give me three good reasons why you own the
company? Let me give you an example. A little more
than a year ago, I began accumulating stock in the
largest thrift in Texas, Bank United Corporation, which
had gone public in the summer of 1996. I was buying
the stock in the mid-20s; as I write this, Bank United
sells around $42. I had three reasons originally for pur-
chasing it:

1. The consolidation of the banking industry was
   still going on, and the big were getting bigger.
2. Senior management consisted of very smart
   people. They could not sell any of their own
   stock for two years, and my sense was that after
   two years they would have ramped the company

up for sale at a premium price to another, bigger financial institution.

3. Home equity loans were legal in every state but Texas, and I believed that Texas would, at some point, pass a law allowing these loans, obviously helping the largest thrift in the state.

4. I had a fourth reason also. I believed that energy demand going into the 21st century would grow significantly and, outside of oil and gas companies, that the banks in Oklahoma and Texas would be big beneficiaries of this development because these states were a center of this industry.

Almost two years later, Texas has approved home equity loans. And my other reasons for owning the stock are still in force. Use this discipline yourself.

Can you give three reasons why you own a stock? If not, you had better question why it's still in your portfolio.

When You Can't Afford to Sell

RETIRED PEOPLE, OR SINGLE PEOPLE WHO NEED income, have often said to me, "I inherited all this GE stock, and it cost me practically nothing. I can't afford to sell any. The taxes will kill me." It may be Gillette that is in your life, or IBM, or another blue chip that pays very small dividend income and that carries a very low cost basis for you.

Seldom do people figure the simple math that can help them resolve their income needs. Let's use the GE example. At this writing, 1,000 shares of GE are worth approximately $100,000. It pays a dividend of $1.40 per share, for an annual taxable income to the owner of $1,400. If you sold the 1,000 shares of GE, assuming it had been held more than long term (one year), and also assuming it cost you zero, the 20 percent federal tax would be $20,000. If you took your after-tax proceeds of $80,000, and you bought, for example, AT&T $8 1/8 percent bonds, maturing in 2022, currently throwing off a yield of 7.8 percent, your income would be at least $6,240 per year. This is more than four times what GE had been giving you. Do the simple math before you decide that you cannot afford to sell something. And don't forget to figure in the state taxes, where applicable. In my opinion, if it's income you're after, selling stock is still a good deal.

Don't Sell Your Winners

YOU'RE NERVOUS ABOUT THE STOCK MARKET. You think it's too high, and you're thinking about selling the Merck stock you bought in the low 30s—since it's now at $120. You say the classic words, "Let's sell it, and when the market drops, we'll buy it back."

Let's assume the Merck is in a taxable account. Say that you sell 1,000 Merck at $120; proceeds before any fees are $120,000. Also assume it's a long-term gain (held over 12 months). Federal tax is 20 percent on your profit, which was $90,000. Also assume a typical state tax on capital gains, which I'll call 5 percent.

Federal tax on the $90,000 is $18,000 (at 20 percent).
State tax is $4,500 (at 5 percent).
Total tax due is $22,500.

Essentially, you have netted $67,500 from your Merck profit after tax. But the stock would have to drop almost 23 points, to 97, to make buying it back worthwhile when you figure your tax costs. And that's just getting you to square one.

Let's assume in these circumstances, I agree with the client, "Okay, we'll buy it back if it drops to $90." Then it drops to $90, and the client typically says, "The stock is acting lousy. Let's wait until it's $85 or so."

Typically, it drops to $87, turns around, and goes to $200. And you've never bought it back. This may be a fictional example of the negatives of market timing, but believe me, it is typical of the thought process. Merck has subsequantly split 2 for 1. If you own a great company that not only should be in your portfolio but also should be in your estate, don't sell it.

Buy more if you want if it drops. But don't sell it because you'll never buy it back.

How Much Should You Buy?

I KNOW A WOMAN WHO IS A GREAT STOCK PICKER. She runs special events for nonprofit organizations, like theater openings and charity balls. With her ability to deal with diverse groups, she comes into frequent contact with many people who run large business organizations. And they tell her about their operations and about their competitors. She keeps her eyes and ears open, and often buys stocks based on what she hears and infers.

Her stock choices are invariably wise. Her problem is that she never buys the right amount of these companies, given her net worth and her long-term outlook. She will say, with $100,000 of money market funds in her account, "Buy 100 shares of XYZ Chemical. It's around $22." She will give me chapter and verse about the merits of XYZ Chemical and why it should be a glorious investment. Her reasoning makes sense to me. She has done her homework, and the stock sells near its 12-month low and carries a yield of about 2 percent. Yet she buys only 100 shares.

This, I find, is the classic mistake of the good amateur stock picker. They get only part of it right. They can choose the right companies, but they almost never know how much to buy. With $100,000 cash and strong convictions about the company's future, I would put 15 percent of my available funds into the stock, buying between 600 and 700 shares. If the stock showed weakness thereafter, and my convictions were still as strong as when I first began buying, I would add, little by little, shares until I had accumulated a total of 1,000.

Making money in the stock market is an art, not a science. Putting 20 percent of your money into a company you have researched fully is not, in my opinion, overcommitting. What you do not want to happen is to be right about a stock, perhaps in a big way, and not to have made a big enough bet to really "cash in" on your insight.

Stocks Go to Extremes— in Both Directions

WHEN A GROUP IS OUT OF FAVOR, IT ALWAYS goes lower than the average person thinks it will. A recent case in point is energy stocks. One of the best run contract drillers in America is Ensco on the New York Stock Exchange. In 1997 the stock sold as high as the mid-forties. Then came the collapse of the Asian economies along with their stock markets, and because of lowered demand from the Far East, coupled with mild winters in our Northeast, energy prices plunged to their lowest in almost ten years. I had thought that in a bad energy stock market, perhaps Ensco could drop, *at worst*, 50 percent or so, to a price in the low $20s. When it subsequently plunged below $15, I began to buy it. Then at the end of 1998, Ensco sold as low as $8 3/4. I continued to buy heavily on the dips, buying stock as low as $9 1/2. Stocks always go lower than you think when they are out of popular favor. *That's* where you eventually prosper. As I write this, Ensco sells around $21.

Conversely, I was buying Merck, one of the great drug companies in the world, in the low 30s when Clinton health care proposals threatened the industry. "It's all over for the drugs, folks," I heard Wall Street analysts say, "They've lost their pricing power." Not for long, I thought, and began buying Merck with both hands, beginning in November 1993. The target I set for myself was $50 to $60 per share, which I thought would take about three years to achieve. When it did hit $60, it went through it like rumors through boardrooms. Today, it sits around $150 per share, only five years later and prepared to split. It went much higher than I originally would have predicted, and I still own virtually every share I bought. (Merck has split and now sits at almost $70, $140 on the old stock.)

The lesson here is to be a cynic. I definitely believe in buying a stock on the way down, when it is out of favor. But never commit all of your available funds at one price. If you want to buy 1,000 shares of something, buy 200 or 300 to start, then average down slowly, on further weakness, to lower your cost price. If you buy something on the bottom, I say that it's probably dumb-ass luck. This game also works when you're taking a profit. If you do hit a target price, sell a little, not a lot. Bleed out your sales as the stock moves higher. It's okay to be a little greedy. And remember, stocks always go further than you think—in both directions.

Consider the Source

TYPICALLY, WHEN I TAKE ON A NEW CLIENT, THE portfolio that comes into me will look fine—with blue chip stocks and a few mutual funds—but somewhere in the mix will be a name like "Renaltronics."

"What's Renaltronics?" I'll ask.

"Oh, some story I got," the new client says, "I forget where; supposed to be a revolutionary product that preserves kidney function forever."

"What did you pay for it? Now it's selling for $1.50."

"Who knows. Maybe I was drunk when I bought it."

When you buy a stock based on a tip from a friend, neighbor, or relative, make sure you stay in touch with the person who gave it to you. It may sound simple, but it is a lesson virtually everyone forgets. When you buy a stock on a story from a friend or relative, *always* remember your source and check back with him or her regularly about the stock's progress.

If you paid $20 for the stock and it declines to $17 and your source says, "I made a mistake, I'm sorry; you should sell it," go ahead and sell it then and there. Do not second-guess your source and figure that someday you'll break even. More than likely, it will decline even more.

You should apply the same standard to the upside. If you have a profit in a stock given you by a third party and you are told to take the profit, do it and be grateful. You took the advice buying the company; do the same thing getting out of it.

When your source has no further information, sell the stock regardless of price. Never fly blind in the market unless you enjoy losing money.

So You Want to Get Rich?

I'M GOING TO INTRODUCE YOU TO A MYSTERIOUS friend of mine, and also help solve the mystery of really making a small fortune in the stock market (as opposed to the saying, "Want to make a small fortune in the stock market? Start with a big one.").

My friend Leonard the Lion is obsessed. He truly cares about only two things: the stock market and, more to the point, his stocks. He's focused the way all truly successful people are focused. We had a drink recently after work. "I had the flu last week," Leonard said. "So I'm lying in bed watching CNBC during the day. What a mistake. All this stuff about the CPI, the Consumer Price Index. It's a laugh. If you watch daytime financial news, you want to go out and shoot yourself. If I wasn't a pro, I'd want to sell every stock I owned. And every bond. Don't people know the true rhythm of life has nothing to do with CPIs? Remember money supply figures ten years ago? That's all you heard on the financial news. And nobody knew what it meant. Then it was fear of inflation. Later it's fear of deflation. Now it's inflation again. All this stuff has got nothing to do with the companies I want to position in the next three to five years. It has nothing to do with my companies thriving."

Leonard the Lion is a wonderful old beast headed for extinction. He has a love for markets, coupled with enormous integrity. He is often stubborn, sometimes profane, and he can dress as if he threw a suit on in the dark. But all the Armani and Gucci in the world can't give you the ability to compound people's money. Leonard the Lion has a client who started investing with him some 20 years ago, depositing $10,000. The account today is worth more than $2 million. Have you got $10,000 and 20 years to spare? Do you have a cast iron stomach and nerves to match? Probably not.

Leonard leaves the office every day at 4:30 and never, ever, carries a briefcase. He also never leaves his desk for lunch and hasn't for more than 30 years in the business, except when a company that interests him comes to town and gives Leonard a freebie. Then he'll have two drinks and eat every course, including the hot fudge sundae; later, he'll go back to the office grinning like a teenager, and get back on the phone with his network.

How does Leonard operate? First of all, he believes in leverage, in margin. "You can't make the big scores in the market without borrowing," he says. "Because you can never buy at the lows. Markets always go against you sooner or later, and you have to be in a position to average down, if you believe in the situation, and you have to own a lot of what you like. A thousand shares isn't going to do it; 10,000 to 25,000 shares is more like it. And you have to be hard-nosed; you can't fall in love. Every day you have to ask yourself, 'Do I really have something here by the nuts?' We've had horrible bear markets along the line while I was building $10,000 to several million. You bet you've got to have the discipline to buy what you like on weakness."

"What about successful traders?" I ask Leonard. "What about beating the market year to year?"

"Forget it," Leonard says. "Traders always sooner or later blow their brains out. I resist the temptation to trade. You take small profits and always miss the big run. And these people who take the quick pops seem to eternally let their losses ride, until it's too late. Never get nervous on action—remember, it's all paper."

"Why don't you sell along the line if you think the market may be going down?" I ask him. "Buy it back later, cheaper."

"Taxes," Leonard says. "You pay at least $6,000 or so tax on a $25,000 profit. Who's to say it's going to go down from $25 to $17? Taxes can kill you. Seldom do people ever buy back what they sell. The pressure is too great to buy something new. Pressure from yourself for the action, certainly the pressure from brokers to create a commission. Brokerage industry number-one rule: Money must never lie idle."

"Leonard," I say, "you're a stockbroker rare in the business. It seems you never want a commission."

Leonard the Lion seldom smiles, so it's worth it when he does. "Don't worry," he says. "I trade against the equity. We've got our large core positions. Sooner or later, they make big moves up, and I use the increased buying power to trade the tape, buy, and sell on short moves. But I always keep the discipline on my core positions. It's the only way to build up your net worth."

I'll give you an example of what can happen if you're a long-term owner of stocks as opposed to a trader. I have a client who had 5,000 shares of NBT Bancorp, which was traded on the New York Stock Exchange. The stock went public in February 1987 at $14, when my client bought it. In the first few weeks, it got as high as $20—a very nice, fast profit. He didn't sell it because he thought well of the management, and he believed in the long-term growth of the area in which the bank operated. When the crunch in bank stock occurred in 1989–1990, NBT sank to $7 a share. Leonard the Lion, if he had been at the controls here, would have reassessed the situation and, if he were still a believer, would have bought more. The Tisches of Loews Corporation were big buyers of banks in those days. My client just held his position, still believing in the solidity and potential for the stock. He originally invested $70,000. At one point, he was down $35,000, but he knew then it was cheap, a mispriced piece of paper.

At the end of 1994, his NBT Bancorp holdings were worth about $240,000, a gain over eight years of 29 percent annually. This did not count dividends on the stock, which that year alone produced $6,000.

Leonard assumes everyone has his zest for the market. With that in mind, here are some of his basic rules for getting rich in the stock market:

1. Do your own research. Use your contacts, and work them. Stockbrokers mostly get stale news, recycled stuff. And company CEOs often are cheerleaders for their own corporations. They wish things were going to be better. They can be the worst sources.

2. Buy at your leisure; never jump with all of your available cash. When your interest is piqued, dip your toe in, buy a few hundred shares. Then you can keep track of it—it's on your screen.

3. Follow people who are winners. Buy what Warren Buffett buys and be prepared to wait. I've followed Kirk Kerkorian for years and always made big money tagging along. The only

time I didn't follow Kerkorian was when it was announced that he had acquired a major stake in Chrysler. I had 5,000 shares in to buy at $11 for myself when my brokerage firm broadcast over the squawk box that our research department said to "avoid Chrysler." I canceled my order, and it was a major mistake. If I had gotten my toes in a little I would have accumulated much more over time. The stock went from $10 to $60, (subsequently much higher) and I never owned it. Follow folks who almost always know how to create value—for instance, the Tisch family, Jack Welch, Sumner Redstone of Viacom, Sandy Weill, the Bass Brothers, Tom Lee the LBO king. They are winners. It becomes public record when they buy. But get your toes into the stocks you want; get them on your screen.

4. If I had a $1 million to invest, I'd restrict the number of companies I'd buy to four. If you're aggressive, you cannot make serious money by spreading it any thinner.

5. Make sure you build up your own account. Do clients appreciate great performance? Not really. The client attitude, and I've been watching this for 35 years, is too often, "What have you done for me lately?" (Leonard is a realist.)

6. I don't encourage a lot of new business; I don't want strangers. I'd attract only sharpies who want an edge, pick my brains, and go to a discounter—

people who say, "The market's up, what's wrong with my stocks?" Hey, I've nibbled at stocks at $15, saw them go to $7, and feeling my way into it, bought more. One I'm in now, Pacific Scientific, did that. It's a lousy market year, right? This year, the stock went over $40, up from $18—a new high, a major score. (After splits, Pacific Scientific dropped from $25 to $10, with Leonard buying all the way down. A year after it had dropped to $10, it was taken over at $30 1/2.)

7. In my experience, stock technicians (chartists) usually buy on the highs.

8. To succeed at anything, be obsessed.

After a few drinks, Leonard offers to drive me home. All he talks about is the market, his babies, and the "program trading whores," who, he claims, have ruined the honesty of the markets. He pulls over near my house and expounds on his theories, not wanting to let me go.

"You should take a vacation sometime, Leonard," I say.

"Are you kidding?" he answers. "Take a vacation when you could be watching the ticker tape? Get a life."

Playing Fads

S TOCK MARKETS ARE SUBJECT TO "FASHION" AS much as the changes in clothing styles. A year or so ago, I had business in New York and went to have a nightcap in the Oak Bar at the Plaza Hotel. At midnight, every seat in the room was taken. Everyone there was drinking various amber-colored liquids, and virtually everyone, male and female, was smoking cigars. Several weeks ago, I repeated the exercise, and only about 10 percent of the tables seemed to have cigar smoke rising about them in pungent clouds. The cigar fad is just about over. Remember, no matter what you perceive as popular in society, be it sneakers, or golf, or comic books, or personal computers, there are groups of stocks or individual companies from which you can profit while the fad lasts.

I have a client who owns an Army–Navy store in Chicago nearby one of the biggest and toughest projects on the South Side. He has made a small fortune understanding fads because, as he has told me, "All fashion among teens in America starts in the black neighborhoods. What these kids are wearing, frankly, is where all the money is going to flow eventually in the shopping malls frequented by the white, want-to-be, copycats who think it's cool to dress like boys and girls in the 'hood.'" Over the last ten years, he has been in and out of Nike,

Adidas, Fila, Tommy Hilfiger, Reebok, and Timberland, among others, getting in early and out as the fickle tastes of the kids changed.

Anything can become a fad or in fashion on Wall Street—the same way women were induced to go for poodle skirts and bobby sox en masse in the 1950s, bobbed hair in the 1920s, miniskirts or hot pants in the 1960s. Wall Street over the years has gone into frenzies over bowling stocks, cable TV, franchising, railroads, antipollution, energy, and aerospace. You name it, and the group has had its day in the sun.

In the last few years, the biggest fad has been the stock market itself, specifically, the Standard & Poors 500, made up of the biggest industrial companies. It has become a knee-jerk benchmark, and few people bother to study a little history about this fad. Recently, one of my best clients dropped by the office, accompanied by a so-called financial planner, a profession that is mostly long on charts and short on experience. The planner was loaded with bells and whistles and graphs showing that the client should have all of his equity money in an index fund that just tracked the popular averages.

"It's foolproof," the planner said. "Low cost and outperforms anything. Beat the street the last two years, and you don't have to think about it."

"What did the stock market do in 1968?" I asked the planner. He shrugged.

"What did the market do in 1982?" I asked.

"What difference does it make?" the planner said.

"Well," I said, "if you'd invested in an index fund, assuming such a thing existed in 1968, you still wouldn't have broken even 14 years later. The Dow Industrials were 1,000 in 1968 and 900 in 1982. Would you be prepared to lose money for your client for 14 years?"

Fads seldom last more than two years whether it's the S&P 500, or Marvel Comics, or hula hoops. If the fad moves into a third year, it is really long in the tooth, and you better be prepared to take some profits and look for the next "hot" area. Does anyone even remember oat bran? Or Davy Crockett? Or the Cabbage Patch dolls? Of course, the Internet stocks are proving to be one of the greatest fads in history. We'll see where most of them sell down the road. If you buy a so-called hot group two years into its popularity, the fad is usually closer to the end than the beginning.

Seeing Beyond the Valley

DO YOU KNOW WHY MOST PEOPLE NEVER MAKE money in the stock market? (I am not counting mutual fund investments in your 401K. I am talking about people buying individual companies for their own accounts.) They almost never make money because they can see prices every day. And it influences them emotionally.

I have a client who thinks he is descended from Napoleon. He is not crazy. Indeed, he is smart in many ways, and wonderful fun because of his interest in unusual things. Like Napoleon, Jim Woods is short and combs his hair over his forehead just like his presumed relative. "My great, great, great, grandmother," he told me long ago, "lived in a little village in Poland. Poltusk was its name. Napoleon won a famous battle there. It's carved in the Arc de Triomphe." Then he rattled on in bad French for a while about the battle, and then back to English. "My grandmother was a teacher, and supposedly was hired as an interpreter by Napoleon. She was a handsome woman, and family legend says that one thing led to another in the emperor's tent . . . and . . . J'ai ici, as they say, . . . here I am."

Jim Woods is the classic emotional investor. He gets itchy in a stock after a year or two of no appreciable price movement, a span of time that regularly wears holders down, and the point at which good things are just about to *start* to happen.

If you're riding a fad, it usually takes about two years for that fad to play itself out. If you're trying to maximize your capital gains, you should try to predict what may be the next fad, or what groups should come back into favor. I like being early because it gives the smart investor time to accumulate a healthy-sized position while most people view your bargain hunting with disdain.

Three to five years is the time, it seems to me, that it takes to produce significant gains, particularly if you are someone who thinks "over the valley."

Your "Stake in Life" Stock

TIME AND TIME AGAIN, I HEAR VARIATIONS OF this story: "I inherited all this Coca Cola stock from my grandfather (or Eli Lilly, or Gillette, or some other splendid company) and I took it to my friends at the local bank. They have a trust department. They told me that I had much too much Coca Cola, that I was too concentrated, and that I had to diversify."

"It's too risky," they said, "to have all those eggs in one basket. Sell at least half of the Coca Cola and spread the proceeds over a variety of investments."

I say this is bad advice.

Fifteen years ago, I was given a perk at my company, free counseling from a very expensive firm that did executive planning. At the time, I had a good deal of my net worth in American Express stock. Indeed, it represented the largest part of my assets outside of personal real estate. After looking over my financial situation, my counselor said, "The first thing you've got to do is diversify. You've got way too much American Express."

"Are you rich?" I asked the young man.

"Well, not yet," he admitted. "But I have high hopes."

"Well," I said, "I'll tell you something my father told me. The only way you can get truly rich in our society is to own a business that can be sold, potentially for a lot of money. No matter how much you make in annual salary, you're going to spend it or have the rest of it taxed. You'll never really accumulate enough to be truly rich. If you don't own your own business, you have to own enough stock in a public company to set you free when, and if, the stock moves up substantially in price."

"I believe in American Express," I told him. "It's tough to kill a great name, no matter how hard management may try to kill it. I don't want to work this hard forever. So I'm not selling any of my American Express. As a matter of fact, I'll keep accumulating it on weakness."

The stock was then around $35 a share. Today, it sells at $125, not counting dividends of 90 cents a share, or the spin off of Lehman Brothers stock, then at around $20, which now has sold as high as $85. So much for diversification.

Years ago, I called this process having a "stake in life" stock. It is your way to create the equivalent (in terms of return on your investment) of having your own company. It is your chance to build a real net worth in the stock market through *concentration*.

For years, every time I saw an enormous portfolio, it was almost always an estate that came in for me to liquidate. These estates usually had a sampling of wonderful companies that had been bought for virtually pennies a share (adjusted for splits), and they had never been sold over many years of ownership. This experience taught me a lesson. You could accumulate great wealth if you bought the best companies and held them, if you did not trade them in for other merchandise.

Refining this further, I believe that to structure the ideal financial life you should identify, as early in your working life as possible, one or two companies that you believe in for the future. I don't care what those companies are, but they should share certain characteristics:

1. They should have universal, global appeal like GE, or Gillette, or McDonalds.
2. They should have instant name brand identification like Coca Cola or Microsoft.
3. They should have products or services that you dispassionately believe will continue to be in demand for years to come; they should be products or services that you and your family find special even over the long run.

Start to buy one of your choices, even in small amounts, through stock discounters so that it is a low-cost enterprise. Have the dividends reinvested in stock if you can. Treat this exercise like a savings account, by adding the same amount every month, or on a special date like a birthday. What you want here, as with prune juice, is regularity.

Every time the stock goes down 15 or 20 percent (and there will be plenty of times like that over the years), buy more. This takes discipline. And the smartest among you, when you encounter these dips in the market, will shout, "Hooray! Now I can add to my stake in life company at bargain prices!"

Your stake in life stock is not for sale, unless some predator takes it off your hands in a buyout. But by then, it will undoubtedly be a long-term capital gain—and you can begin your hunt for the next gem. A very few stake in life stocks should form the core of your holdings. Everything else builds around this core: bonds, preferred stocks, the common stocks you will buy and sell at various times.

Of course, the more of something you hold, the higher the risk. But as a wealth-building strategy, concentration over time, with well thought out companies, can set you free.

Betting on Winners

THIS SOUNDS SIMPLISTIC, AS WILL ROGERS once said, "If the stock isn't going to go up, don't buy it." But there are CEOs of companies who only seem to make money for themselves and never make it for the stockholders. And there are people who make plenty for themselves but take everyone around them, including the stockholders, along for the ride. Of course there are Warren Buffett and Bill Gates among this group. And Sandy Weill of Citigroup, (my parent company). And Jack Welch of GE, Harvey Golub of American Express, and Lou Gerstner of IBM are proven winners who create value for others. Ted Turner has also, jump starting Time Warner when it was stuck on hold. And I'd watch Amos Hostetter coming into AT&T with MediaOne, and Strauss Zelnick, head of BMG Records wherever his career leads him. These are people who truly add value, and there are not many of these who can deliver the goods for people other than themselves.

Never be embarrassed about picking the best brains. It is a talent in itself, and is, of course, always an education. When it comes to the stock market, however, you have to learn to differentiate between people who seem to make money only for themselves and people who thrive personally but who almost always never spread the wealth.

I had a friend years ago who left the investment business and moved to San Francisco in the mid-1970s. Eugene has always been a charming hustler who could sell anything to anybody. He went West to take over a woman's apparel company that was publicly traded. "Why the hell should I buy the stocks when I can go out and buy the companies?" he reasoned. He took the dress company and merged it with at least six different companies in different industries from cosmetics to toys, and claimed he was building a "female-oriented conglomerate juggernaut."

Eugene's stock, constantly promoted by him and his public relations flacks, ran from 3 to 33. Along the way, he sold millions of his own shares, which he had acquired for pennies in stock options; grabbed more millions through salary, bonus, and perks; and assembled a modern art collection worth millions more. But, despite his wealth, he remained a hustler and insecure. Every time he met someone new, he recommended his stock and always used the classic hustler's line. "Do yourself a favor," he'd say, "buy some for your mother."

My wife and I, on a visit to San Francisco, had drinks in his apartment high above the city on Telegraph Hill. When we were enthusiastic about the art scattered throughout the place, he uttered a line destined for the Insecurity Hall of Fame.

"This stuff is all right," he admitted, "but you should see what's in storage." His juggernaut collapsed eventually, and Eugene went on to other companies, looting them systematically, but doing nothing that was ever deemed illegal. If anyone ever tells you, "do yourself a favor, buy some for your mother," run, don't walk, in the opposite direction.

Buying into America's Most Hated Companies

I F YOU'VE BEEN READING CAREFULLY, YOU KNOW now that I often believe in going against the grain of popular investment thought. I believe in being a contrarian. If you take this route in investments, or in life itself, you stand the risk of being very wrong, sometimes for long periods, until the crowd finally turns your way. But when it does turn, as I keep emphasizing, prices almost always go much higher than the average smart person could predict.

A classic example from several years ago is the drug stocks, vilified and shunned by most of Wall Street, when Hillary Clinton and Ira Magaziner were conspiring (from much of the investment community's perspective) to put the pharmaceuticals out of business.

I was buying Merck in the mid teens (now $70 or so) and Bristol Myers in the teens as well (now almost $70), when Bristol was yielding in the 5 percent range on its dividend alone. "How can you be buying the drug stocks?" clients asked. "They've lost their pricing power. It's all over."

"Open your eyes and look around," I said at the time. "I'm getting at least five calls a week to look into long-term health care (nursing homes and the like) for my clients or their parents and grandparents. Demographics say that the elderly are growing exponentially in number; they all take drugs in increasing amounts, and they're living longer. Every day the drug companies introduce new remedies for what ails us—and it's a whole lot cheaper to take a pill than to be hospitalized."

"Don't get so excited," my clients would say. "You'll have to take a pill."

"That's my point," I said. "And I'm excited because I can buy these companies so cheaply." When the drug stocks turned higher, they have probably gone much higher than, as I said earlier, the average smart person would have believed. Merck, for example, has more than quadrupled in the last four years.

When certain stock groups fall out of favor, the reverse is true: They almost always go lower than even smart people would imagine. Over the years, knowing the psychological nature of market behavior, I always try to nibble at my favorite areas, buying them slowly and holding cash back to take advantage of even lower prices if they occur. For instance, if I like a beaten down stock, and it's selling for $20, I discipline myself to say, "I am going to buy a total of 1,000 shares for myself." I start by buying 300 shares.

Invariably, one never buys at the lowest point unless it's, as I call it, "dumb-ass luck." Usually, the stock will trade lower later, and I will add to my holdings, gently, sometimes 100 shares at a time, until I lower my cost average and eventually accumulate my 1,000 shares. (If you have an investment portfolio, always make sure you have flexibility, meaning some cash on the sidelines. If your funds are completely committed to the market, you cannot add to your holdings when you see lower prices.)

What usually happens to the most hated companies? Usually a catalyst comes in, most likely in the form of new management that intends to revitalize the dormant company. In the last several years, this has happened to IBM, American Express, Time Warner, and AT&T—all companies that were reviled on Wall Street but that turned out to be major winners if you had accumulated shares during their years in the desert.

In the last year, in my opinion, we had a chance to look at a current favorite among the most hated group: energy stocks. With the slowdown in the Far East economies, oil and gas companies had been hit fairly dramatically in the last several years. The rationale is that demand for energy would decline along with the economies of the Pacific Rim countries and that the slowdown would inevitably spread to Europe and the United States. This, coupled with warmer than usual winters, had led to oil prices declining from $22 or so (per barrel) to approximately $11 before a recent bounce. Lower prices for the product equals, in all probability, lower stock market prices for all energy-related companies, drillers, refiners, exploring and equipment manufacturers. In my opinion, the slide had been overdone, with some stocks down 70 to 80 percent from their highs of just several years ago.

My energy guru lives in Grand Bahama, "because of the weather and the taxes," as he explained to me. Franco the Energy Maven is an iconoclast in the best sense of the word. We do not generally love honesty, not when it comes from our friends or relatives nor when it's spoken in board and committee meetings. Because honesty can be confrontational, it can seem hostile. And most people avoid it at any cost. "You look fabulous," for example. "We've got to have lunch soon. Or dinner, better yet," for another example. Honesty takes so much work.

"The more honest I was," Franco told me years ago, "the more I would lose jobs, board positions, wives. So, I dropped out of hypocritical society. Of course, it helps if you've got your f—- you money, which I have. I've also got a lot of perspective on the world because any number of honest people, meaning other cynics with their own f—- you money, sooner or later swing by Grand Bahama.

"Let me tell you why you have to back up the truck and buy oil and gas stocks. In China, they consume one barrel of oil per year per capita. In Taiwan, just a few miles away, they consume 11 barrels of oil per year per capita. In the United States, it's 25 or so barrels of oil per year per person. In ten years, if China even goes to two barrels of oil a year, the world will need another OPEC to serve it. And there ain't another OPEC."

"What about electric cars and/or fuel cell–operated vehicles?" I asked.

"Ha," the Maven scoffed at me. "Anything practical on this front is years and years away. Look on your roads: vans, Jeeps, trucks, guzzlers. Zero conservation policy, zero energy policy, except to use it up. Back up that red Chevy truck and buy the energy stocks."

It doesn't take a genius to see the potential in energy stocks. Use your common sense. Everywhere on American roads, you see sport vehicles, Jeeps, minivans, Range Rovers. I know people in the suburbs who have bought Chevy trucks (usually red). They go mall shopping in these trucks; tossing bags from Gucci and Neiman-Marcus onto the flatbed. One friend told me, "Hey, I actually carried 50 feet of hose in my truck. Am I a farmer or what?"

Everyone forgets those days when Honda Accords were on allocation and every driveway in Beverly Hills had one as a status symbol parked next to the Rolls or the Bentley. My clients in Los Angeles called these Hondas, "my dinghy."

I also agree with Franco on demographics. George Olah, a Nobel Prize winner, recently remarked in the

Wall Street Journal that there are six billion people in the world today. "We will be ten billion in thirty years and all of them need energy," he pointed out.

The chairman of Exxon has forecast that in the next 10 to 12 years, Asia will consume more oil than the United States and Europe do together. In my opinion, you won't have to wait that long. Markets always anticipate the future, right or wrong, and energy stocks should be accumulated when the investment world finds them out of favor.

What's the smartest way to do this? I favored a three-pronged approach:

1. Start accumulating energy blue chips like Exxon, Mobil, Chevron, and Royal Dutch. Have your dividends reinvested in stock, and use these companies as savings vehicles. You can do it also with the big equipment manufacturers like Schlumberger. If they decline by 10 percent, add to them.
2. Buy a sector mutual fund that specializes in energy. Again, be prepared to add to your holdings on dips, and be disciplined about it.
3. Establish your own "vulture" fund (see Create Your Own Vulture Fund).

These first two approaches are conservative methods for playing an area you think represents value. The third is a more aggressive approach.

Create Your Own "Vulture" Fund

Y EARS AGO, MY FATHER USED TO GO THROUGH the list of American Stock Exchange companies and cull out 10 to 20 cheap Canadian oil and gas companies, whenever energy stocks were out of favor. These stocks all typically sold for under $10 a share. He would put out a memo to clients listing the companies and say, "Buy these stocks as a package. If you buy 100 shares apiece (or 1,000 shares apiece, etc.), it will cost you X dollars. My prediction is that if you buy the package of 20 companies (for example), at the end of 3 years, 5 of the companies will be bankrupt, 5 will be about the same, and 10 will be double or triple or more from what they sell for currently."

When the energy cycle shifted, uncannily, my father's method always worked. Call your financial consultant, or establish a relationship with one and ask for a list of their current favorites in modestly priced energy stocks. Call half a dozen brokerage firms and ask for any research list they may have. If you see any energy recommendations duplicated at different firms, put them on your list.

This strategy works if you are prepared to wait several years for extraordinary returns. If you used this method in the early 1990s with bank stocks, for example, you could have made the score of a lifetime, and with blue chip banks as well. For instance, in 1990, the Bank of Boston sold as low as $3 a share. Three years later, it was $12 a share. After only 8 years (and you all know how quickly time passes), Bank of Boston sold as high as $120. Make your own vulture fund list from areas of the market that are in disfavor. You can get rich in stocks if you dare to bet against the herd.

The Next Big Thing

FOR SEVERAL YEARS NOW, EVERYONE WHO HAS come into my office as a new client has had the some complaint: "How can I get anyone to pay attention to me in a society that doesn't seem to give a damn?" They complained about health care, their banks, their plumbers and carpenters. They complained about 800 numbers, rudeness, traffic. They complained about their children and their parents. They complained about technology.

Underlying it all is the fear that society is becoming, has become, increasingly anonymous, and that it seems tough to find anyone who cares. One woman, a widow, said to me, "When I grew up we knew everyone in our hometown, and ten people in the next town. People stayed in the community; they married and worshipped in it as well. Now, everything is so fragmented. If you have three or four children, they could marry white, brown, black, pink, and blue and be scattered to the four corners of the earth. Frankly, it makes me nervous and it makes all my friends nervous also." These people were not seeking investment advice as much as they were seeking refuge. Clearly, today, there is an enormous opportunity to separate yourself from the crowd in this increasingly anonymous society.

When I drive into my building's parking garage in the morning, the day manager usually comes at double time out of his office and flags me down. When I was new in the garage, he would tell me, every day, where there were empty spaces so I could move directly to the appointed level without hunting. After I got to know him, he would save a space for me right next to the elevator, no matter how crowded the garage was.

His name is Haile—he came here from Ethiopia, highly educated and motivated, and bearing the name of the longtime emperor of that country. Haile means power, he has explained to me, and he often shows me his ring, which has the lion of Judah on its bezel. "That's me," Haile always says, and I believe him. He treats everyone with eagerness and enthusiasm, and he makes the experience of early morning a treat because of his energy and good humor. Haile has been offered a dozen jobs that I know of by people in the building: law firms, investment companies, consultants. The more he turns them down, the more he becomes intriguing to them.

"I'll know when it is right," he tells me. "Sooner or later, I will move on." Everyone in the building wishes that all of their employees were like Haile and that they gave half the energy that he brings to everyone, every morning. I've asked him about this, and he has said, "My father was a great example for me. He taught me that whatever you do, you do it with pride, and if you do the lowest of jobs in this way, people will notice and someday you will run the business."

"Your father told you this?" I asked.

"Everything but the last part. I learn this in America."

What Haile offers is the key to prospering in the new century. It is called adding value, going above and beyond what is expected. It is also a surprise, and should be, for people on the receiving end of the added value. Why does Haile save a space for me daily, next to the elevators, when there are more than 200 spaces in the building? Because I have asked him about his life, his childhood, his impressions of America, and his memories of Ethiopia. All the occupants love Haile's care of them and their cars. But not many people bother to find out who he is. Adding value can work both ways.

Value added essentially makes you say, "They didn't have to do that." It makes you notice people and corporations that surprise you by giving you more, or better, than you expect.

For instance, if you want prime examples of greed and entitlement in society today, professional athletes would be high on everyone's list. At least in ancient Rome, these entertainers fought to the death, so there was some weeding out. But today, we have to hear them whine and complain and go through the motions until they can blissfully retire, then sign autographs at sports memorabilia shows.

On the other hand, John Havlicek has been named one of the 50 best professional basketball players of all time. I played golf with him recently in a friendly game. It was the first time I ever met him. On the first tee, he took the shaker of grass seed that sits next to most tee boxes and filled in all the divots (tears in the turf made by golf clubs digging in) created by other people. This is rare indeed among golfers, many of whom do not appreciate the gentlemanly aspects of the game, including respect for the course, but in a professional athlete, it is *highly* unusual.

Too many of them believe that life is a continual free ride with little responsibility for their behavior. During the course of the round, Havlicek told me that his family were butchers in Ohio and that in early childhood he remembers not having indoor plumbing—and how often his parents carried neighborhood workers through bad times, extending credit, and helping the community. "I never forgot those times," he said. "So when I had good fortune, I was a saver. I didn't want everything I had worked for to be taken away by bad times or foolishness. And the harder I worked, the luckier I got."

Later in the round, I asked him what he thought the most important quality was in leading the successful life. Without hesitating, he said, "Patience." Prodding him to explain, he told me, "If you believe in yourself, and keep coming on, you will triumph. When I played with the Celtics, we knew we would win every game. And when we lost, it was because, and only because, we ran out of time."

John Havlicek retired in 1985, and he planned well for his time in the sun—but what you remember about him is the extra dimension. You know that he's a world-class athlete. But you'd want to hire him for your company, whatever your company might be doing, because he's a surprise, a world-class gentleman. Value added. Of course, I would put a little asterisk on the scorecard whenever I outdrove him. Three times. But what you really remember is the guy who repairs other people's divots.

Looking for value added should be an integral part of your security analysis as well. You can do your digging in this regard, without any help from Wall Street. I'll give you several examples of how you can prosper from the value-added concept.

I have a client in Dallas who is a high-stakes gambler. Jerry Joe travels the world from Vegas to Macao looking for the edge. When he invests in the stock and bond markets, he looks for the edge as well. To Jerry Joe, this means, "make an investment because you are thinking about 'what happens next' if I do this."

He gave me an example some months ago when he came to town to scout out some opportunities. "In Houston, my wife runs a small bookstore connected to our church. The store handles several hundred titles. You pay full retail; no discounts, and it'll take about two weeks to get a book for you they don't carry. There are three women working in the store, and they are passionate about books. They will help you because they read everything and will recommend titles. Or you can go to Borders or Barnes and Noble about a block away. They stock thousands of titles, mostly at 20 percent off, all automated and glitzy, not personal at all. But if you go online with Amazon.com, you have access to two and a half million titles, delivery in a day or so, and big discounts. Plus they give you reviews and interviews with the authors. They'll also give you your choice of gift wrapping, showing you the choices right on the screen. Watch this stock when it goes public," he added, "it's what everyone longs for today. But finds so tough to get . . . value added." Amazon.com went public at around $5 per share, adjusted for splits, and sold as high as $221 in the spring of 1999. Since then the stock has declined, but partly because of competition. Others are getting the "value added" message.

I have come across several more recent examples of this quality in my own empirical research. At a political fundraiser, a large crowd, I ran into the chairman of Staples, the office furniture superstore chain, which is growing internationally as fast as it is growing in this country. Staples sales are over $5 billion and they employ upward of 32,000 people. "I'm a pen freak," I told the chairman.

"Most people don't tell me their innermost feelings at political fundraisers," he said.

I reached into my jacket pocket and pulled out three different ballpoint pens. "I love pens," I said. "And I can't find any medium points anywhere. Only fine points. It's driving me nuts." He took out a small notebook and his own pen.

"I'll bet you that's a fine point," I said. He checked it, nodded his head, laughed, and moved on into the crowd. A week later, a small package arrived containing a dozen medium-point pens from various makers, and a note. "This should satisfy your cravings for a while. And, thanks. Our conversation made us look at our entire pen picture for the first time in a while. Enjoy." It was signed, Tom Stemberg, Chairman of Staples.

I own the stock. If you get this attention to detail from the person who runs that large an organization, what do you think it says about how he wants his customers treated? Everything starts at the top, good and bad. Think about this when you buy stocks for your own portfolio. Staples has gone (adjusted for splits) from $7 5/8 in the last few years to a high recently of $34 1/4. This is no accident.

Last winter my wife and I were at a cocktail party in what my wife calls, "02138." This is the zip code for

Cambridge, Massachusetts, also known as "The People's Republic of Cambridge" in various publications around America. After a few glasses of clear liquid over ice, it wasn't so bad—even though academia is almost always more poisonous than corporate boardrooms. It's not enough that they use knives, they're usually tipped with poison, "or dung," a professor told me once, "just like Pungee stakes in Vietnam." After a few conversations that were more name-dropping contests than anything else ("Madeline Albright checked in the other day; Steve Breyer looks wonderful; if Kissinger begged me on bended knee I still wouldn't give him the time of day"), I chatted with Marshall Carter, the chairman of State Street Corporation, the nation's largest processor of mutual fund transactions. I have my checking account there although they function as a traditional bank more as an accommodation than anything else. The real money is in their custodial services. "I bank in one of your oldest offices," I said to Carter.

"Everyone responsive to you there?" he asked.

"Yes," I said. "But I do have a small gripe. Your checks were always heavyweight, substantial checks, meaning the paper seemed solid, like the bank itself. You've changed vendors in the last year, I think, and the quality of the checks themselves has gone way down, in my opinion. They're like tissue paper. I would bet you've received a lot of complaints." He didn't say. But he took my card and made a few notes. The next morning, the phone rang at our house at 7:30. My wife and I were having breakfast. A man introduced himself as a vice president of the State Street Bank and told me, "Marshall Carter e-mailed me and said you had a problem. What can we do to solve it?" Boy. I hadn't even put the raisins on the Grape Nuts yet and the State Street Bank wanted to work with me on the quality of their checks.

Look up the stock record for yourself. In the last few years, State Street has gone from a low of $33 to as high as $95. This is no accident, either. Good things are going to happen to your own pocketbook if you identify companies that deliver more than they promise, or you expect, and buy the underlying stock. It's the next big thing.

Betting on the Generation Gap

IF YOU'RE LUCKY IN LIFE, YOU WILL KNOW, AND BE friendly with, people who are older than you. Perhaps it's someone who trained you early in your career; perhaps it's a teacher with whom you remained in touch; perhaps a coach or a mentor from your job.

Henry the Red is a philosopher, a flaming redhead when he became a client years ago. "I'm a garmento; a cloakie," he announced to me then. "I make maternity clothes, a noble profession. I invented the motto for our business, too, because if you're a cloakie, you have to be prepared to do everything. The motto of my business is, "You knock 'em; we frock, 'em." Henry the Red loved to trade the market. He was not very serious about making money; he just wanted the action, and one more person to whom he could pour out his often outrageous ideas. Now Henry the Red is winding down, his hair thinning and fading gently like a rich watercolor painting that has just been allowed to take on too much sun.

I use Henry the Red as a sounding board, partly because he has an opinion on virtually every subject. And he delivers those opinions with absolute certainty. Some time ago, for instance, I happened to ask him about discounts and deals. "You want to learn about discounts and deals?" Henry asked. "Well . . . a woman goes into a grocery store and asks the owner for the price of a pound of sugar. 'Eight cents,' says the grocer."

"'Eight cents!' says the lady. 'Across the street the man is charging six cents.'"

"'So why don't you buy it from him?' says the grocer."

"'Because he's out of it,' answered the lady."

"The grocer smiled in triumph. 'When I'm out of it,' he said, 'it's only four cents.'"

"But I don't want to philosophize about money," Henry the Red said. "You've got to have it. Period!

Essentially, I believe what George Bernard Shaw said in *Man and Superman*, 'lack of money is the root of all evil.'"

Henry the Red knocked his pipe into an ashtray. "For the rich," he said, "anything is forgivable. For example, I'm a nogoodnik if I have guests at my house and I excuse myself to go watch Dan Rather. It's rude. But I have a friend who did some business with J. Paul Getty, at the time the richest man in the world. He was over at Sutton Place, Getty's palace outside London, and in the middle of cocktails, Getty excused himself. My friend was left alone in a room the size of Bridgeport, Connecticut, and a butler came in to ask if my friend required anything.

"'Mr. Getty left so abruptly,' my friend said. 'Was there anything wrong?'

"'Oh no, sir,' said the butler. 'Mr. Getty excuses himself every day at this time to watch his favorite show on the telly.'

"'What's Mr. Getty's favorite show?'

"'Oh, sir, it's that animal adventure,' said the butler, smirking. 'Daktari.'"

Henry the Red reads everything, watches everything, and now, at 81 years of age, is spending a lot of his time on the Internet. I picked him up recently to take him to lunch. He wanted to go to his favorite delicatessen.

Along the way, he dropped the following observations: "Life is a business and you're the CEO." And: "The person who makes the company go is the guy who creates the product." And about partnerships: "There has probably never been a partnership in history where the partners didn't basically hate each other."

"Just bet on older people," Henry tells me. "There are over 75 million baby boomers facing retirement in the next 30 years. Social Security will absolutely be privatized, meaning part of it—billions of dollars—going into the stock market. The pressure is building, and it won't be resisted any more than communism could resist capitalism once it saw all those consumer goods shining at them on television from our satellite broadcasts.

"And when you can put a piece of your Social Security funds into stocks, you'll be restricted in your investments into the biggest and best companies. Uncle Sam doesn't want you fooling around with your retirement in junk. So I figure that AT&T, Pfizer, Procter & Gamble, the best known names, will double or triple on this new infusion of billions of dollars."

The restaurant seemed shabby and badly in need of paint. But Henry the Red was greeted by everyone, owner, waitresses, and other patrons, as if he were a visiting celebrity. He nudged me with an elbow when he saw my hesitation. "Don't you know," he said, "that a true deli is no good unless it's dirty?"

Boring Is Better

DON'T THINK THAT YOU HAVE TO INVEST IN high technology to invest in growth. And don't think that companies that pay dividends cannot be growth stocks. The opportunity of a lifetime existed in the early 1990s when bank stocks—stodgy, old, horribly managed, boring bank stocks—had virtually all imploded, plummeting in price, many down to single digits. The Bank of Boston, for instance, got down as low as $2 per share. It had recovered to over $120, before a 2 for 1 split.

Why is this? In simple terms, the perception of the business changed, the Federal Reserve loosened credit, the S&Ls were punished, insolvent banks were closed, and the consolidation of the banking industry began. From thousands of independent banks in America, we are moving toward having only hundreds of banks.

The same thing is going to happen in the utility industry, and in the energy area, with competition increasing and consolidation on the march. This revolution is in its early stages, but the perception of boring utility stocks will be changed forever within the next decade.

Boring really can be better. It surely beats seeing your software favorite miss analysts' projections for the quarter by a penny and plunge 30 percent in a morning when the institutions all head for the door at once. With utilities, you'll also collect some income while you wait for the action to happen. I like to be paid while I wait. Never dismiss any group as boring—when value starts to move, it can produce extraordinary results.

When Bad Things Happen to Good Stocks

EVERY ONCE IN A WHILE, WHAT WE THOUGHT were good ideas turn to dust. Either conditions changed too quickly or you underestimated the length of time a trend was in place or you took at face value what was told to you by people who should have known better.

In the stock market, there are numerous examples of this, and there is not a money manager in the country or an investor to whom this has not happened. In my own life, I have seen this happen most often when people fell in love with their stocks and knew stubbornly that they could not be wrong.

One of my friends owned Bank of New England heavily at around $15 a share, after it had fallen from the

30s, in 1989 and 1990. "Insiders, the directors, were buying the stock at $20," he told me. "The Tisch family, who control Loews, are billionaires. They're buying banks with both hands—Bank of Boston at $15, for instance," he said. "This crunch in bank stocks is overdone."

Remember this: When a trend is in place, it almost always gets overdone—in both directions. He loaded up on Bank of New England at $15. Then more at $10. Then even more at $7, and went on margin at $5, convinced he had gotten to the bottom.

The stock went to zero, when the Feds, overreacting in the climate of the times, and some said, politically motivated, closed the doors of the bank. Bank of Boston also, despite the investments of brilliant people like the Tisches, went as low as $2. The bearish trend in bank stocks ran way beyond what most intelligent people thought it could. The reverse was true as well, as banks reorganized and skyrocketed in the 1990s, with Citibank for instance, going as high as $175 from the teens. If only. . . .

So what do you do when your best idea turns to dust, when your net worth becomes seriously affected by a declining stock in which you have a large position? My friend, Practical Paul, has been in the investment business for more than 40 years. "And I've got the scars, the ulcer, the triple bypass to prove it," he tells me.

I bought him lunch one day recently at his favorite restaurant, a greasy spoon located down an alley in our city. But Practical Paul likes it because they have wonderful meatloaf sandwiches on thick rye bread—and

Scotch whiskey at lunch for $2 a pop. He has two of these every day with his meatloaf sandwich. "Here's how I play disasters in my portfolio," he said. "First of all, you have to really be honest with yourself about what kind of a company you're stuck in. Is it IBM that went from $175 to $50 and got new blood to turn it around, or is it National Student Marketing that went from the hottest stock in America to zero because management was horrible and the concept of kids running the world went down the toilet? If your disaster is basically a good company," he told me, "you can employ several strategies." He then mentioned a few of them:

1. I accumulate more of the stock at desperate prices to try to cut my average cost per share way down, and I employ patience, the true investor's greatest asset.

2. I double up on my disaster stock, and 31 days later, sell the original shares to establish a loss. You'd be amazed how many so-called smart people never use this technique. It works like this: I own 1,000 shares of Possum Systems at $40, and I believe the future is bright for this company. But demand from the Far East dwindles, earnings temporarily tank, and the stock goes to $20, a 50 percent loss. But I still love the company, and I want to keep my holdings intact. However, it's a long way back to $40. If I sell the 1,000 shares, I can take a tax loss on the stock

and use it to offset other gains, or carry the loss forward, perhaps giving me a nice tax advantage. And then I can buy back the same number of shares 31 days later. This way you can both establish a loss you perhaps can use and maintain the same number of shares you originally had, but at a much lower cost basis. (You must wait this time, according to tax laws, to buy back a stock after taking a loss. Or else it doesn't count and is treated as a "wash sale.")

3. You can implement these ideas, and you can also "strategize" around the problem. In my own portfolios, while waiting out a stock I am sure will work eventually, I will often start to accumulate a "cheapie" that I believe in, that is, a stock selling under $10 a share, sometimes even under $2 a share.

This is a very risky method! Some will say it's akin to putting a chip on black in a casino, and, when the little ball rolls into the red hole, doubling up the bet on black, and on and on until the gambler eventually wins. Of course, I'd like a nickel for everyone who has gone broke on that system. Here's how it ideally would work in the stock market—this is an actual illustration from my own investment life.

I owned a stock that had what the company felt was revolutionary technology. I owned the stock, call it 1,000 shares, around $20. My assessment of the company's basic business was that it was worth $20 a share without the potentially revolutionary new product, and that the basic business would protect me from disaster if the new product didn't work. The new technology imploded, for various reasons, and the stock declined fast to $10, cut in half. The key to good stocks that go bad is, do not be frozen at the switch. React to problems; develop a plan.

Now I had $20,000 invested in my "revolutionary" stock with a $10,000 loss. To balance this, I bought 3,000 shares of an energy stock at approximately $3, spending $9,000 plus commissions. My plan was to work around my technology problem, waiting for it to recover while my cheap oil and gas stock (which I thought was a real value) made up the slack.

The rest of the story, as Paul Harvey would say, is like life itself.

I did buy more of the technology company at cheap prices, and a year later, it was taken over around $30 a share, and my disaster turned into a triumph. During the same period, my energy stock went from $3 to $7, a major score.

But as I said, this money business is like life itself. I never sold the energy stock, and it declined to under my original $3 cost. Now I have to strategize around *that*.

I *could* recommend to all of you Leonard Bernstein's brilliant musical *Candide*. Voltaire (the author of *Candide*) was appropriately cynical, and the musical mirrors this. One of the songs reflects my strategies and frustration often by the circular nature of money. The lyrics say, in part something like, "What's the use, what's the use, all this getting and fretting, if it winds up upsetting, and wrong, so very wrong, if you just pass it along."

I don't want to pass it along. We're in this to make money. If you make a mistake, even if it's temporary, make sure you're not frozen at the switch. And make sure you have (or whoever watches your money has) a plan.

Marketplace Bellweathers

THERE IS A FAMOUS STORY, PERHAPS APOCRYPHAL, about the stock market. Supposedly, in 1929, Joe Kennedy, the founding father of the clan, was having his shoes shined on Wall Street. The young man doing the shining was holding forth on his own market performance and his current favorites.

Kennedy went right from his shine to his office and (as the legend goes) sold the market short heavily and made a killing during the crash of 1929. The obvious lesson is that when the shoeshine boys are playing the market and winning, it's time to head for the exits.

Everyone who watches other people's money has his or her favorite superstitious signals for tops and bottoms of market cycles. I have had dozens of clients over the years who think they are unique in saying, "You want to make money in the market? I have a foolproof formula . . . just do the opposite of everything I do." These people, of course, are trying to ward off the evil eye by saying this. They don't really mean it, and they aren't really signals for the top.

Signals come from people who act contrary to their usual behavior. For instance, a woman in Oregon, a client of mine for 20 years, called me when the Dow Jones Industrial Average was flirting with 10,000. She had never called me in 20 years. Her husband, a doctor, has always checked in, assessing the health of the family portfolios.

"I've never taken much interest in finances before," she said to me, "but I've just joined an investment club and I'm curious about some issues." I'm curious, too. And happy that she's becoming interested—but at 10,000 on the Dow? This sudden interest after all these years was a classic sign of being close to a top. Then, in the summer of 1998, I saw people whose children were out of the house who were moving from the suburbs into the city. And because of the growth of their stock accounts in the past few years, they were priding themselves on paying more than the asking price for houses and condos.

One man, who moved into town during the last few months, offered $250,000 more than the asking price for an apartment in a sealed bid situation. "Hey, location, location," he told me. "If it's a primo building, I can't ever lose money."

American's more than any people on earth, forget pain as soon as it disappears. From 1990 until the last several years or so, you couldn't give apartments away, or commercial space at premium prices. All memory of gas lines, recessions, wars, the daily obsessions with money supply, or the Nikkei average are gone. We are natural optimists, which as a natural characteristic, is wonderful. But never say never, or this time it's different. It's not you. Look for your bellweather signs and act on them. Of course, late summer and early fall devestated markets in 1998.

When money seemingly has no meaning, and is being thrown at goods—whether houses, art, or common stock—it almost always means we are heading for a painful adjustment. It's just a question of when. Remember, trends run much longer in both directions than the average person thinks they will.

Signs of important junctures in markets correspond with people's irrational mood swings and with sweeping pronouncements like, "IBM will never come back,"or "American Express can never recover; it's over." Same for Chrysler, the banks, the drug companies, Union Carbide after Bhopal, Con Edison after it cut its dividend long ago, and endless other stocks once pronounced dead. Another classic sign of a top: The investment business and consulting are the current first career choices for graduates of Harvard Business School. Remember that human nature never changes; it's only the buzzwords that do.

Buying on the News— Part I

I T WAS THE DAY AFTER THANKSGIVING, AND I WAS staying home, visiting with family in from out of town and hoping to play golf if the weather was not too chilly. The stock market was open, and my office called me about 10:30. It was Sardonic Sandra, my chief assistant. "Mr. Emotion called this morning," she said. "He saw an article in the paper about a new prostate cancer drug being approved by the FDA. Company named 'Men's Health' has the drug. Mr. Emotion wanted 1,000 shares. Said he didn't care what he paid. It closed at $10 on Wednesday."

"What did he buy it for today?"

"He paid $13."

"Does he know he paid 30 percent higher than Wednesday?"

"That's your department," answered Sardonic Sandra.

My client, who we all call Mr. Emotion, is often whipped into a frenzy by the media. He believes everything he hears and reads. In his professional life, he is a labor lawyer, wise and full of common sense. As an investor, he was made to be taken, the kind of person traveling carnivals were invented to exploit. My role was to calm him down, prevent him from fiscally blowing himself up. Occasionally, I would be on vacation or out of town on business, and he would go wild, a junkie with a fistful of dollars and a wicked habit. He would sell IBM at 55 because of negative press (it went over $300); he would buy Presstek at $125 because he "heard they were going to revolutionize printing" (it dropped to the teens). He would sell Bank of Boston at $5 because "all the banks are going to zero" (it moved to the $100s before a split) and buy at the top of most fads in the marketplace from oat bran to HMOs. Here are a few rules for trading on news stories:

1. First, by the time you read the news, it's usually too late to take advantage of it if you're buying. And too late to sell it if you're selling.
2. If there is outstanding news on a company you want to buy, and it closed the day before the news came at 10, put a limit order in to buy it. This means buying at no higher than a specified

price like $10 3/4 something you are willing to pay. If you place a "market" order in to buy the stock, as Mr. Emotion did, you run the risk of paying (as he did) 30 percent higher than yesterday's price. (The $13 he paid.) If it opens higher than your limit of $10 3/4, you wait. Inevitably, after the first burst of enthusiasm, it will come back to your price. "I was a schmuck," Mr. Emotion said when I contacted him. "I wanted it at any price."

"Anything you will pay any price for," I told him, "you are doing for reasons that have nothing to do with that price."

"Like sex," he said.

"Most likely," I answered.

Put limits in what you buy on good news. Sooner or later, maybe $13 would prove to be cheap for the cancer drug stock. But sooner or later, as Lord Keynes said, "We are all dead."

3. Selling on bad news is a little trickier. I was a big buyer of Union Carbide years ago when the explosion at their plant in Bhopal, India, blew up in a major tragedy. The stock imploded from the 60s to the 30s. If I had owned it in the 60s, I probably would have added to it on the way down. Markets often give us a chance to buy cheap merchandise, when good companies are out of favor, or somehow get onto the most hated list, like Union Carbide, or IBM, or

American Express under Jim Robinson. This is where the money is made if you're patient. When bad news breaks and a stock tumbles, try to focus on what you think the future really holds for that company: Does it fill a niche? Can new management change the picture? I have almost always made money averaging down on quality companies, buying on bad news. Bad markets can be a boon to the serious investor. It allows you to buy more of the companies you love to own.

Buying on the News— Part II

M Y WIFE AND I HAD A WONDERFUL FRIEND, Peter, who died much too soon. He was a consultant, primarily to defense contractors, and he always said that, "what keeps me sane is knowing that the world is mad." He would call me at odd times, always with an unusual comment. "Where are you?" I would ask him when he obviously sounded as if he was on a cellular phone.

"I'm stuck in traffic on the San Diego Freeway," he would say, "but I am enjoying myself."

"How so?" I would ask.

"I'm reading over my prenuptial agreement."

After I had known Peter for a few years, I said to him one day, "Did you see that article about the Russian Mafia in the *Wall Street Journal*?"

Peter replied, "I haven't read a newspaper in 20 years."

I was shocked. "What do you mean?" I said. "You're basically in the information business. How can you not read the papers?"

"Well," he said. "Twenty years ago I knew all about two things. And every time I read about those two things in the newspapers, they always got it wrong. So I figured, if they're wrong about what I know, how about what I don't know? So, I save myself about 2 hours a day, and I haven't read a newspaper in 20 years."

Everyone I've told that story to at first laughs. Then they say, "You know, he's absolutely right. No article I've ever read about something I knew has ever been right on the money." Of course, this is why you have to do your own analysis of any financial reporting in the press.

But the first rule to remember when reading financial-related news stories is that most of the time this news is already reflected in the stock's price. Most of the time it's old news to those who try to anticipate both trouble and positive developments.

When energy stocks are out of favor, invariably bearish stories surface in the press. The same is true for entertainment stocks, housing stocks, paper company stocks, and bank stocks. Yes, it even happens with computers. When times are bad, there are endless tales about why "it's over." I remember taking a major position in the parent company of *The Boston Globe* (Affiliated Publications), in 1990 when real estate markets in Boston and the Northeast were in severe recession and it looked as though all the major banks were closing their doors. I was buying the stock between $7 and $9 a share. Clients called when they saw what I was buying and said, "Everything I read tells me that newspapers are dead. No one will read them anymore." And "Don't you know we're in a depression in Boston?" And "Newspapers? How boring can you get?"

Did you know that newspapers are the first place to show recovery as an area moves out of recession? Because classified ads pick up. And a city like Boston always will recover because brainpower moves to this city for the schools, the hospitals, the high tech, the biotech, and the mutual fund industries. Harvard and MIT are not moving to Kansas. The Mass General and Beth Israel Hospitals are not moving to Utah. And *The Globe* had a virtual monopoly on the region. Within several years, *The New York Times* bought *The Boston Globe* at $15 a share, part cash and part stock. And in about five years *The New York Times* stock moved up from the 20s to the 70s. So much for conventional wisdom.

There are two things to learn if you watch media coverage of your industries and companies:

1. When the news is continually bad, you have to consider if this could be the bottom. Watch the list of new lows weekly. This is where there could be bargains. And remember the classic media call: A cover of *Business Week* in the early 1980s that trumpeted "the end of equities?" It coincided with the beginnings of the biggest bull market in history.

2. Consider good news. Usually, by the time good news breaks, the stock price already reflects this information. There are always people who know these things before you do and are selling their shares to you as the news breaks.

A neighbor of mine, a psychiatrist, saw an item in the financial section of the newspaper about hopeful cancer research by a local company. The article was published Friday morning after Thanksgiving, and because this is historically a quiet day in the markets, the stock did not really react to the news. Sunday, as my family and I arrived home from the weekend, our neighbor came running from his house. He was breathless. "You've got to buy this for me," he practically yelled. "First thing Monday. It's a major breakthrough." He was waving the article.

"My advice to you," I told him, "is never buy on inflammatory news. It takes time, usually a lot of it, for discoveries to be absorbed, and the value of it will take years to spin out."

"Fagettaboutit," he yelled. "I know what I'm talking about. Just buy it." It had closed the previous Friday around $12. The psychiatrist paid $15 1/2 on the opening on that next Monday. It got as high as $15 7/8. Two weeks later, it was $10. If you have to buy a stock on news, buy half of what you originally intended. Then, on the inevitable sell off, after the initial enthusiasm, complete your original buy order and lower your cost. You will almost always have a chance to buy your favorites at cheaper prices, and you want to make sure you have the funds available to do it. Don't spend your entire wad at one time and at one price.

Buying on the News— Part III

ONCE IN A WHILE, BREAKING NEWS CAN signal the beginnings of a new move in a stock, not the top of an old move. Sometimes, momentum caused by a breakthrough—in a product, an invention, a process, or a new drug—can roll the stock upward for years.

Sex, strangely enough, can often be the catalyst that produces this "long wave." In the 1960s, Syntex Corporation developed the birth control pill, which transformed the lives of all of us forever. "The pill" changed attitudes about dating that still reverberate today. All through high school and college prior to the pill there were two major concerns for young men: "Will I ever get it?" and "If I do get it, will she get pregnant?"

One of my friends, who had married his high school sweetheart and had been wed for some time when the pill was introduced, looked around the bar where we were having a drink. It was 1964, and he pointed at all the young men and women noisily enjoying themselves. My friend slammed his glass down, knowing he was missing the sexual revolution. "God damn it," he said. "The world is several billion years old. And I was born five years too soon."

Syntex could have been bought on the news of the approval for sale of the pill to the public. Its rise went on for years because the momentum of the implications of the product rolled on and on. This may be true as well for Pfizer's new anti-impotence drug, Viagra, approved by the FDA and marketed originally in the spring of 1998. *Barron's* said that sales are predicted to reach $1 billion by its fifth year and also estimates that "20 to 30 million men in the U.S. may suffer from the problem." The pill may also improve the sexuality of women, particularly older women who have had problems during intercourse. Pfizer then sold at around $98 a share, and on the surface, it did not look cheap. During the last few years, the stock sold as low as $41, and carried a price–earnings ratio of 58, with a current yield just under 1 percent. This is seemingly not the bargain counter. But everywhere I went, I heard about the subject. Some months ago, Sardonic Sandra, my assistant, who takes everything with a grain of salt, said to me when I came into my office, "Call the Pervert; it sounds urgent." The Pervert, as Sandra calls him, is an eminent psychiatrist, Dr. Weiss, who specializes in treating academics, mostly ivy leaguers who teach in graduate schools. Sandra calls my client the Pervert because his biggest clinical interest seems to be in the sex life of his patients, and, when I'm not in, he converses with Sandra about his findings. He had made a big hit with Vivus, a NASDAQ stock, and its product Muse (Medicated Urethral System for Erection). I am *not* making this up.

When I called the doctor, he said, "I had to speak to you. I'm so excited. Do you know there are almost 50 million men in the world who suffer from impotence?"

"Is that all?" I asked. "Why do you plant this seed in me first thing Monday morning?"

"Because you watch my money, and you should share my joy. Buy me another 1,000 Vivus at $40 or under. This stock is going to $150. At least."

I told him, "I've heard that Pharmacia and Upjohn's injections work better than Vivus." (Vivus's drug is placed into the urethra in the form of tiny pellets.)

"You want to stick a needle into your Johnson, fine by me," said the psychiatrist.

"Look," I said. "I don't have a problem. We're talking about stocks."

"You don't have to get defensive with me. I'm the doctor."

I put his order in, thinking that discount brokers didn't have to put up with this. They were merely order takers. But I am in the business of therapy, and the doctor went with the territory. I found Sandra and asked her, "Why couldn't you ask Dr. Weiss if he wanted to place an order?"

"He got angry with me if you want to know the truth." She was looking sheepish.

"Okay," I said. "Come clean. Why was he angry?"

"I just told him a joke."

"All right," I said, "let's hear it."

Sardonic Sandra began. "Well, it's about my friend Bernie. He was having trouble with impotence. So he went to his doctor, who told him there was a new, revolutionary pill, and that if you took it, it would give you an instant, giant erection for 20 minutes. Bernie was thrilled. 'Give it to me now, Doc—I'll run right home and surprise the wife.' So Bernie takes the pill, and *boinng,* immediate success. He jumps in his car—it's the middle of the afternoon—and races home. The cleaning woman is there, but no wife; she's out shopping, the woman tells him. Already he's lost ten minutes. He begins calling stores to find his wife. Nothing. Five more minutes is gone. He panics. Two minutes left. He calls the doctor in a frenzy. 'Doc,' he says, 'two minutes left. It's amazing, but my wife is out shopping.'"

"'Who's home with you?' the doctor asks."

"'Just the cleaning woman.'"

"'Well, try it with her; it shouldn't go to waste.'"

"Bernie hesitates. 'Doc,' he says, 'for the cleaning woman, I don't need a pill.'"

Vivus is now selling around $4 a share, and the new buzz surrounds Pfizer. It sure seems much simpler to take a pill than any other means of solving the impotence problem.

I had a dinner meeting a few months ago with 12 men, 5 of whom were more than 70 years old. All of them were fascinated with the possibilities of Viagra, and although there was much posturing and ribaldry, I had the distinct impression that if there was a 24-hour drugstore in the neighborhood, all of my companions were going to make a bee-line right for it.

I met an older stockbroker the next day, and he expounded on the same subject. "At last," he said. "It's okay to talk about sex in the office and get away with it. Put on a straight face and discuss the various merits of the pill. One of my buddies, by the way," he went on, "tested it and claims it changed his life. This is going to be huge. And I can talk about it to every woman in the office. Legally." I told Sardonic Sandra about this, and she said, "Boys and their toys . . . but I think we'd better take a serious look at Pfizer." The stock subsequently went up over 50 percent. Not one man I've met anywhere during the weeks that followed failed to bring up this subject.

So, when good news breaks, ponder whether it's something everyone already knows and likely to be the end of something, or whether it's news that could just be the beginning, an investment theme that you can capitalize on for years.

Selling Short

I'M AN OPTIMIST. I BELIEVE THAT GOOD THINGS can come out of bad events. This includes the stock market. I have some 1,700 clients, people living all around the world. No more than one of these people ever sell a stock short in the space of a year. Why is this? Americans are optimistic people—they like betting *for* things, not against them. They particularly like betting on themselves. "I don't like wishing for things or people to fail," is a typical comment people give when asked about short selling.

But short selling can be an invaluable tool in your investing repertoire. Short selling is the mirror image of buying a stock (going long) and hoping it appreciates. If you buy 100 shares of a stock at $20 and sell it at $30, your profit is ten points, or $1,000 before taxes and fees. If you sell 100 shares of stock short at $30, you borrow 100 shares from your broker to deliver to the buyer. If it drops ten points, you buy it in, closing the transaction. Then you deliver the bought-in shares to the broker you borrowed from. It dropped ten points, and $1,000 profit is credited to your account (again less eventual taxes and fees). Professional traders short stocks all the time.

Here's how you can use this technique. You know you want to own superior companies like Procter & Gamble, Exxon, or J. P. Morgan. And you hope you prosper with those companies for years. And you occasionally want to own companies you have a strong feeling about because you use and like their products or services—Ralph Lauren (Polo), perhaps, or Staples, or Starbucks.

What if you have a bad experience with a company, its products or services? If you reward good companies by becoming a co-owner (with other shareholders) and buying their stock, how about "punishing" corporations that don't fulfill your expectations? Most of the time, your instincts—good and bad—will be shared by others, and the stocks you admire will eventually go up; the stocks you don't will decline.

Do not spend your life looking in the rear view mirror of "shudda, cudda, wudda . . . didn't." Here's a situation, like hundreds you may have experienced.

Recently, I bought a computer for my business, a Compaq with various bells and whistles. I was advised by my staff about the products, and they purchased everything from CompUSA. The total bill was $2,700. After the equipment was delivered, it seemed the PC was missing a sound card. Could we get CompUSA to address the problem? After five days and numerous waiting on hold for almost half-hour stretches, after endless runaround and buck-passing, we finally got a live person. "Tell them I'm canceling the order," I told my crew. "Let them come and pick it up." When we told them we were canceling, we finally got service.

But the experience was disenchanting to say the least. I could have bought a computer in a dozen places. So if it were only service they were selling, my eyes and ears told me that CompUSA was a disaster. I could infer that if I were having problems with CompUSA, probably many other people were in the same boat. I told my staff, "I'm going to pay for the computer by shorting CompUSA stock."

I sold short 500 shares at $35 a share. And within three weeks covered the stock, closed out my short position at 28 for a profit of approximately $3,500. Yes, of course I have to eventually figure in the tax on my profit. But the point is I turned a bad experience into a happy and profitable one. And I had a good story out of it as well, a psychic victory that I could share with others. "Let's go for the laptop now," I told my crew, and when the stock ran up again to $36 or so, I shorted 600 shares, covering again around $31 in less than two weeks. We're getting there, as far as the laptop is concerned. But I'm probably not going to short the stock again for myself. You have to be careful about being too greedy.

I had a purpose shorting CompUSA. And I had a target. Only a few months after I covered the shorts, the company announced disappointing earnings, and the stock sold down to the high teens, and eventually under $6. But the principle was the lesson here. You can profit from businesses that disappoint you.

Trading on Instincts

I BELIEVE IN TRUSTING YOUR INSTINCTS IF YOU trade in the stock market, not in trusting your brother-in-law who gave you a tip, or in the news media that report on the financial world. When I sold short CompUSA for myself, I did it on instinct, admittedly, looking for a quick hit. I really did no research beyond a practical eyes-and-ears approach to the transaction. Do not expect miracles or fortunes from these types of trades. You may get lucky in the short term. But never commit long-term money to a situation unless you have really done your homework. (I did not sell any CompUSA short for clients.)

But I will give you a general rule if you ever think stock markets are too high. In greedy markets, if you honestly think prices are much too risky to buy, then sell short the stocks of the stock brokerage firms. As stock prices fall, revenues generally fall at the investment firms of America as well. The brokers fall faster than practically anyone else in bear markets, and this is as true of the well-run firms as it is of the marginal ones.

Borrowing to Beat
the Squeeze

LIFE IS NOT FAIR, OF COURSE. THERE ARE TIMES when the world is bright, when the baseball looks as if you can count the stitches while it's floating to the plate, or the 20-foot putts magically drop in, when your skin is taut and your smile brilliant and you can't lose. That's when the world will, it seems, grant you any wish. Much of the time, of course, our shoulders droop, we miss the three footers, and our confidence erodes.

Likewise, when you desperately need money for taxes, or tuition, or any other pressing reason, you may feel the need to sell your stocks to raise the cash. Unfortunately, when you need to liquidate almost anything, you'll always get the worst prices. Your stocks will be at fire-sale prices. I call this predicament the "squeeze syndrome."

Most people who own homes have mortgages. And they have credit card debt. Seldom do people who have stock and bond portfolios have any margin debt resulting from the borrowing against their accounts. But this borrowing can sometimes be a very useful tool.

Say that you need $15,000 for a tax payment and you have a $100,000 portfolio of stock and bonds. I might say, "Don't sell anything now to raise the $15,000. It will diminish the value of your holdings to $85,000 and probably result in capital gains taxes on what you're selling, a double whammy. Temporarily borrow the $15,000. You can borrow up to half (50 percent) of your portfolio value and get the funds immediately if you sign a simple margin agreement."

All debt is not necessarily bad if you can be smart about it and keep it under control. If markets are temporarily down, and my clients need cash for various emergencies, I sometimes recommend that, instead of selling securities, they temporarily borrow from their own accounts, getting the cash they need, and strategize to repay the loan at a later date using assets that once more have appreciated. Yes, you do pay interest on the loan, usually a point or so over the prime rate. You also get tax credit for your margin debt against any interest or dividends you receive. So, theoretically, if you get $1,000 in dividends, you can offset those dividends against $1,000 of margin interest. And you continue to receive all the dividends and interest on your investments; what's more, you retain control so that you can pay down your debt balance when you see fit, on an orderly basis, as your portfolio recovers.

Red Flags

VIRTUALLY EVERY TIME YOU SEE A NEWS ITEM about a public company that has either fired their accountants or announced that their accountants or auditors have resigned, it is time to sell that stock. On the same tack, every time you note the resignation or termination (firing) of the chief financial officer of a public company, it is time to sell the stock.

Don't second-guess this move; sell it immediately. In my experience, the numbers are almost always suspect in assessing companies' prospects. Companies can do amazing things with their books. When the auditors leave, or when the CFO exits, more bad news usually follows. Eventually, the stock may be a buy, but in the time it takes to straighten out the mess, you could be using your money in much more profitable directions.

Making Money on Stock Splits

I AM OFTEN ASKED, "DO I BUY BEFORE OR AFTER a stock splits?" I believe in buying before the actual split. But playing stock splits properly requires understanding the psychology of investing, the head part of the game. One of the main reasons for splitting a stock is that the average person avoids high-priced securities. Many people won't buy a $100 stock because it seems out of reach. But if it splits and sells at $50, it seems that much more attractive. And people like to buy 100 shares, round lots. It makes them feel good.

People like to wait for the lower, post-split price, but it often costs you more if you wait. With so many people in the U.S. stock markets today, money is extremely itchy. And the media get the herd extremely excited. With so many watchful investors jumping in when the newly split price occurs, there is inevitably an immediate jump in the price right after the split.

For example, if you had 100 shares of Lucent in the winter of 1998, when the stock sold for approximately $80, a two-for-one split would have given you 200 shares selling for $40. (In theory, the overall dollar value would be the same, but you'd have twice the number of shares.)

In fact, Lucent's price jumped from around $80 to over $120 after the split was announced in the press. And within days of the actual split, it jumped from $62 to as high as $73, or a price—figured before the split— of $146. Look at what you missed if you waited for the lower price before buying. My rule of thumb: The day you get the announcement that a split is pending, buy the stock. It split again in 1999, two for one, at a lot higher price.

You can act even earlier in this process if you really want to make money and are honest with yourself about having patience. Look for stocks that sell above $100 a share. Inevitably (other than Buffett's Berkshire Hathaway, which he claims he'll never split), the board of directors will split the stock to make it more attractive to the investing public. It took me under 5 minutes to scan the New York Stock Exchange tables and identify at least 15 companies that fill this bill. Even if you bought odd lots of all 15, chances are good that you would eventually own round lots (more than 100 shares) of all of them.

Trading on Inside Information

I PLAYED GOLF IN A TOURNAMENT LAST SUMMER. IN one of the matches, an opponent was playing particularly well. The man a stranger to me. After a few holes, he told me that he was famous, that he had been taken away in handcuffs in one of the insider trading scandals of the late 1980s. He told the story as if it were his badge of honor, as if he had to keep telling it. "My mother in law," he laughed, "kept telling my wife how she had never trusted me." After he told me the story, I finally remembered him. But I couldn't help watching him in the rough, couldn't help counting his strokes on each hole.

"You cannot legislate human nature," my father used to say, particularly when he was talking about

Prohibition, the period 1919 through 1931 when the sale and consumption of alcoholic beverages in America was forbidden. Whether government likes it or not, we all want to feel that we're on the inside, that we have the true scoop on what's new, what's hot, and above all, what's secret.

"When I first came into the securities business," Ed Hanson told me, "in 1925, every morning the senior partner, Charlie Helliwell, would come down the stairs from the partner's meeting and say, 'Boys, time to buy some United Fruit!' And it would always go up because he was given the word. Almost everything we did was inside information from the partners who were all connected to their clients at the major corporations. Those were the good old days."

Ed is still on the payroll at 90 years old, and he has guided me through many crises in my career by telling me stories like the following:

"Joe Kennedy, the founder of the family, did business with us. I was in charge of running out for him to buy cigars when he was low. He'd tell me, 'Kid, it takes a long time before people listen to what you say and think they're getting something special. When you get a reputation for making money, you can say, rub cold cream on your middle finger and massage it into your temples. It helps your concentration.' If you have money, or people think you have, they believe you know everything about everything. Suckers. Knowing human nature is better than knowing when Big Steel is going to raise their dividend. Knowing human nature is the secret to riches. And it pays not to take anything at face value."

Ed Hanson can't make it into the office anymore. His brain works perfectly, but his body betrays him. "CNBC has kept me alive for the last five years," he says on the phone. "I can watch the tape (the ticker tape), and turn down the sound when the pitiful stream of Wall Streeters parade their nonsense. Give me Joe Kennedy any day. People chasing the pots of gold today will mostly wind up with chamber pots. Study human nature is still my advice to you. If you want to thrive."

People have been calling me for years with inside information. In my experience, the information is wrong almost 99 percent of the time. And the 1 percent that is right never happens when it is supposed to happen. It always takes much longer, and it is almost never with the company that was supposed to swallow Corporation X.

But people still go to extraordinary lengths to take shortcuts. I know a man, whom I call Nervous in the Service Nelson, who believes that there is a giant conspiracy out there to prevent him from ever making any money. "Hey," he said several years ago, "Get this. I'm renting next door this summer to a guy doing deals with Anthony O'Reilly, the chairman of Heinz Foods. My neighbor is going to Pittsburgh all the time where Heinz is located, and I'm sure O'Reilly is going to sell out the company at a big price." Nelson tells me how he enlisted his wife in his hunt for inside info. "I told her to ask the guy's wife for drinks on nights that I was in the city. Wait till she was on her second glass of wine and ask her where her husband was traveling to that week. I knew that if it was Pittsburgh all the time, we were in Fat City, especially if it were on weekends. When people work weekends, there are deals in the works. There would be a deal for Heinz." Nelson goes on.

"When I'd come down to the rental, I'd go through the trash. We shared the same barrels, kept in a little shed," Nelson told me. "And who is going to rip up memos in the summer? I'll reemphasize the tip," Nelson said, "that almost always holds up. If bankers and top management have weekend meetings, it almost always signals a deal in progress. If the meetings take place over Memorial Day or July Fourth weekends, times the wives will be really pissed off, it's certain to be a deal. I call the investment bankers' offices late on Fridays of holiday weekends, tell the assistant that I'm supposed to play golf with the chairman on Saturday, and ask if there is some kind of a screw up. You'd be amazed how often the assistant or secretary tells me exactly what's going on."

Almost every rumor you hear about takeovers has some basis in truth. Yes, the company probably has had fishing expeditions launched at them, people who may be interested in acquiring all or part of a corporation. But more deals fall through than go through. And one thing is for sure: The company you buy because you think it's going to be taken over may very well be taken over, but never when you think. It may take years. Or it may never happen. I ran into Nervous in the Service Nelson a few weeks ago.

"Nelson," I greeted him. "You gave me Heinz as a sure thing five years ago, and it still hasn't been taken over. What kind of inside information is that?"

He grinned sheepishly at me. "I got out of that a long time ago. My next door neighbor caught me going through his trash."

"And?"

"We can't go to that summer place anymore. Besides, I've been kicked out of better places. Currently, I'm trying to get close to American Express. There have been rumors for months."

I had a client once who tried to date the daughters of CEOs of public companies. He had a twofold plan: Either get inside information from the dating process or get offered a job with the company. As long as there is greed, there will be people looking for an edge, and looking, by hook or by crook, to beat you to the punch. We all want to be on the inside. If you do your homework, or have someone working for your money who does his or her homework, you will get your share of takeovers. And you will get them by intellectual hard work, not by sifting through trash.

Do your own homework on your stocks. If you follow the rules in this book, you won't need to get your neighbor's wife drunk either.

Never Reach for Yield

WHEN LONG-TERM 30-YEAR TREASURY notes have a current yield of approximately 6 percent, as they do while I'm writing this, there is a tendency, particularly on the part of retired people, to say, "I remember, not so long ago, it seems, when government bonds were 12 or 14 percent. What happened to that? Try to get me higher than 6 percent. I need the income."

This is when I start to hear about instruments yielding between 9 and 12 percent: master limited partnerships, junk bonds, foreign issues, pipelines and timber, liquid natural gas and fertilizer—mostly highly sophisticated investments that are unintelligible to the average investor.

In my experience, here's what happens. The yield-hungry investor buys a high-yield (junk) bond paying 12 percent, and pays par for it ($1,000 per bond). Everything is fine for a year, and the income is wonderful. But after holding the bond for 12 months, the company that issued the bond files for bankruptcy. The bond plummets to $50 ($500 per bond); the investor has lost half of his or her money on paper; and the bond ceases to pay interest while the company goes through a reorganization and the lawyers take charge. So the investor goes from a risky 12 percent to zero on the income side, and sees his or her principal drop by half as well. Very few people really understand the high-yield markets. If you're dealing with them, be careful.

When you are offered almost twice what conventional sources (for example, Treasuries) yield, it is often too good to be true and potentially dangerous to your financial health.

Private Investments

I T'S EASY TO BUY 100 SHARES OF EXXON OR Microsoft. Public companies are available to everyone. Private investments are a different story. Here's a brief primer to this side of the investment world.

Unfortunately, life is not fair. We all know this. And we also know that sometimes it's unfair in our favor. Many private investment firms ask for a minimum investment of $1 million or more, although several Wall Street firms will wrap together the monies contributed by many people and invest for you as part of a package. Even then, the minimum investment is at the $500,000 mark. These could work out fine, but pay attention.

Thousands of investors, thinking they were half-assed rich in the 1980s, and much too heavily taxed, poured hundreds of millions into so-called tax shelters, which promised instant deductions, or writeoffs, sometimes in multiples of three to four times the actual investment. Then, many of these promotions claimed, down the road, after the major tax deductions had been take, the investments would grow over time into long-term capital gains, taxed at lower rates than ordinary income.

There were oil and gas deals, real estate partnerships, barges, low-income housing (known as Section 8s), movies, and endless others. And the public couldn't get enough of them. When the tax laws changed in 1986, followed by the stock market crash in 1987, and then the real estate and banking crunch in 1989 to 1991, virtually all these "tax shelters" disappeared, imploded.

Yes, people got tax deductions (though phantom income later surfaced in many deals to bite people in the tail), and they also got to write off almost their entire investments in these packaged products.

What the public clamored for in the 1980s, they massively sued the investment community for putting them into it in the 1990s. Dirty pool in my view. At the time, the customers demanded the products; Wall Street packaged the demands, taking exorbitant fees, and it all turned to dust.

Caveat emptor, say I—let the buyer beware. I'd be willing to bet that no investors at the time, nor any of their accountants, either read or understood the prospectuses that accompanied these deals. If they had, the fees alone would have scared away anyone with half a brain. The syndicators grabbed with both hands.

I have a rule of thumb about deals that people try to sell me, and it involves the "plop factor." Someone in the newspaper business years ago told me that he could always tell how the newspaper business was by dropping the Sunday paper on the floor from waist height. The bigger the "plop," the bigger the classified section, and the bigger the profits. I drop prospectuses on the floor: The bigger the plop, the more lawyers are involved—the more lawyers, the more fees, the more fees, the worse the deal probably is for investors. Drop your prospectus on the ground; the bigger the plop, probably, eventually, the bigger the flop.

Venture Capital

I MET BILLY BOYD ONE DAY ON MY WAY BACK FROM lunch. The back entrance of my office building is surrounded by steps leading up to a kind of vestibule where workers come to stand out of the weather and smoke. Billy was wearing a blue double-breasted suit with a gray chalk stripe, and he was showing a group of bicycle messengers gathered on the steps how to play baseball against the stairs with a red rubber ball. He could throw the ball time and time again against a point on the marble stairs, which launched the ball repeatedly over the narrow street to the sidewalk on the other side. "Are you a former messenger?" I asked him. He whipped the ball at me sidearm, and of course, I bobbled it, but didn't let it get behind me. "Good field, no hit," I said to him, tossing the ball back underhand. Billy walked with me into the lobby.

He introduced himself, saying, "I know who you are. I read your stuff." He was in the midst of closing a deal and visiting one of his many lawyers. Billy did deals for a living, seeking out opportunities that he felt others hadn't even thought about yet. "That's why I was fooling with the messengers, asking them who was busy in town, where the most deliveries went, what they watch on television, what music they listen to, what they're doing on the Internet, if anything. If you do deals, you have to listen to the old folks, the young bloods, everyone. If you don't, and you miss a demographic group, you are not doing what you should do. You don't want to say, down the road, 'I should have thought of that.'"

Billy was really into cable and cellular phones, and very simple concepts got him interested. "People wanted to be in touch with their offices when they were stuck in traffic," he told me. "It was as simple as that. With cable,

I thought that essentially, people wanted good TV reception. And it grew from there. I went to trade shows, walked around and met people. I got to know commissioners in Washington. I targeted these industries and became an expert. Society changes so quickly, and I always remembered the words of Cooney Weiland, for many years the Harvard hockey coach. It's great advice for spotting trends. Cooney said, 'Send me hockey players who react. There's not enough time to think.'"

What you should seek out in life are people who are obsessive, compulsive, and are leaning on these qualities in your behalf. When Billy was researching cable TV, among other assignments, he was sent to Alaska. "The key to cable," he said, "is simple: Count the houses. I did it wherever I went, and I asked to see every complaint file to see what we needed to do the most." Billy, among other triumphs in his life, got a corporation to put up $12 million into a company producing new technology. That investment ultimately became $5 billion. "I believe that life is circular and that the circles meld into one another. So cable becomes the Internet, for example. You always have to be seeking the next circle."

You cannot read the financial press today without seeing stories of hundreds of millions of dollars being raised for venture capital funds and leveraged buyouts (LBOs).

A leveraged buyout firm invests in the mature phase of existing businesses that seem to possess upside and unrealized potential. Then, after the investment has been made, the LBO firm orchestrates the turnaround. There is a lot of leverage in this type of operation. An LBO firm might have committed an actual $5 million of their own to a $300 million deal. If they can grow the company to $400 million, you can see how leverage works in their favor, plus fees they take for managing the money the investors have poured into them, typically up to 2 percent of assets under management plus 10 percent of the gains. The best-selling book *Barbarians at the Gate* told the story of the classic leveraged buyout: RJR Nabisco—the restructuring of an existing company.

A venture capital firm invests in the startup phase of companies, or even in pre-startup situations, nursing and grooming these startups through the growth phase into the mature phase and eventually bringing the company public. Venture firms invest in stages; LBO funds go in once, and concentrate on putting in the best CEO, and often new management, to fulfill their agenda. Most of the great high-tech firms were originally funded by venture capital companies: Intel, Microsoft, Dell, and America Online, for example, along with all of the Internet startups.

After knowing Billy for a while, we would play golf together several times a year. During these sessions, he would share the secrets to his success in private investments:

1. *Scared money never wins; it's always afraid it's going to be taken away*. Think about this one: My father,

for example, never got over the Great Depression. He beat it into me growing up that "you had to save for a rainy day," that you mustn't owe any money, that life was going to hammer you when you least expected it. He found it difficult to live and enjoy life because he was constantly looking over his shoulder for the next depression.

He repeated these themes so constantly that I was determined, when I grew up, to spend, travel, and live. And if it were all taken away from me, at least I would have attacked life in some small ways and be able to say, "Yup, I did that. I saw that. Before they took it all away from me."

Looking back at all this, I am surprised at the attitudes of that generation who were so colored by the Depression. During this period, my dad was in his early 20s, a time in people's lives where, if things go wrong, there is endless time, a long life ahead to come back, or thrive, or change things. If bad things happen to you in your 20s or 30s, and if you're willing to work hard and be positive, you will succeed; you can turn it around. If you want a model of how to lead an extraordinary life, read William Manchester's introduction to his book about Winston Churchill, *The Last Lion*. The introduction recounts a day in Churchill's life at

Chartwell, his country estate, prior to World War II when his countrymen had written him off as finished, an aging fool who didn't count anymore. This was before he became prime minister and emerged, in many minds, not just mine, as the most important person in the 20th century. The reason for this digression is to underscore Billy Boyd's first dictum: "Scared money never wins."

2. *In every deal, there's a "pink Cadillac," and you'd better find out early in the deal what it is.* "Years ago, I was buying a radio station in Louisiana," Billy told me. "The seller was getting nervous."

"What's wrong?" Billy asked him.

"Well," he admitted, "my wife is upset at me." He was sheepish, and somehow I felt the deal slipping away."

"Tell me about it."

"Well," the owner of the station said, "Every year we buy her a new pink Cadillac. . . ."

So, Billy immediately wrote into the agreement that the wife would get a new pink Cadillac annually.

3. *You should always back people in venture deals, not products.* People who back products usually lose. In the venture business, it's people; in the LBO business, it's bringing the right person in. The great investors understand human nature better than they understand anything else.

4. *Technology takes longer to develop than anyone might think*. Years ago, I read a book called *Goodbye, Gutenberg* that implied, among other things, that nobody would read newspapers or magazines any more, and that everyone would get their news off the TV or computers. Well, I don't see too many people taking computers into the bathroom with them, do you? The snail darter may be endangered, but books, newspapers, magazines, are very much alive and well.

   It's like the prediction that the 21st century will belong to China. This may be absolutely true, but it may take until 2036 or 2045 for it to become apparent. A lot of people will both die and go broke waiting for this to come true. And these days, for many investors, three months seems like a long time.

5. *People with something to hide also make the best investors*. Insecure people, so conscious of their own image, are great at judging people. You understand what you're trying to hide, so you tend to detect it in others.

   Several years ago, I owned a large position in Tambrands, a company that manufactured basically one product, Tampax. I participated, after I was deep into the stock, in a small meeting with the then chairman of the Tambrands board. The chairman seemed so uncomfortable during this session that I had the distinct impression that he, if asked, would not describe what their only product actually did. I guessed he would either sell the company or take it down the drain. He did the former, thank goodness. But I always thought he sold it much too cheaply, just so he wouldn't have to tell anyone what he did for a living. If this implies *I'm* insecure, and I spotted it, big time, in him—so be it.

6. *You should judge venture capital firms from where they get their money.* In my opinion, it's good strategy to follow wealthy families and universities into investments. This method isn't foolproof, but by and large, these funds are the smartest and the best. And they can pay smart people to do their due diligence for them.

7. *In assessing companies, get to know the receptionist.* I'll sometimes ask a receptionist, "What does this company do?" You'd be amazed how many times the receptionist has absolutely no idea. When this person does know, and tells me lucidly, I know the company communicates well. It is the little touches that give you a feel for whether you invest in it or not.

The first time I tried Billy's dictum, I was waiting to see an agent at one of the largest and most famous of Hollywood/New York's talent agencies. "What does this company do?" I asked the young lady.

She looked at me as if I were nuts.

"Huh?" she said. "Who do you want to see?"
I never signed with that agency.

8. *I believe, in small companies, the optimum Board of Directors size is five people.* I would choose only one person from the company; two financial people whose role should be a continuing process of raising funds; one industry expert for obvious outside expertise, and one throwaway person chosen to provide comfort for everyone else.

9. *Hire the brightest people you can find.* Ted Williams wasn't trying to make money; he was trying to be the best. It's the basic reason why you should own Microsoft. Think about it: 10,000 of the smartest people on the planet e-mailing each other all day with innovative ideas. How can you beat that?

Billy Boyd likes to come up to my office unannounced and putt golf balls into a glass that he lays on the carpet. He brings his putter with him, and I always have golf balls around my office—presents from clients, promotions from people eager to sell me something. He putts for a while, then he goes over to my west-facing window that looks out over Beacon Hill and the Charles River and the Back Bay. "I came up here to look at Fenway Park," Billy Boyd says. "It's a reality check for me, the dreams of childhood." He pulls a red rubber ball out of his backpack, the same kind of ball he was playing with, with the bicycle messengers outside my building. We play catch in my office.

"Why am I playing catch with you, Billy?" I ask him. "In the middle of my life in the middle of my busiest day?"

"Because," he said, "you believe I am going to significantly add to your net worth. And because one of your flaws is wanting to find out how things come out in the end."

"It takes one to know one," I answered, whipping the rubber ball back at him, which he caught with one hand.

Billy still guides me through the venture capital universe. I know that his basic principles of life also extend to his business. Billy says, "Loyalty is everything. I like to think of people in a battle in a bunker with me. Whom do I trust to protect my back?" He also has told me that he pays attention to how people in power treat the least of their followers, when they think no one is watching. And above all, Billy keeps emphasizing, as he goes from deal to deal, "scared money never wins."

Investing Abroad—Part I

IT IS TOUGH ENOUGH INVESTING IN YOUR OWN backyard. Why punish yourself putting your money where your mouth isn't? In my experience, people have generally invested overseas because of the buzz in the media or the financial press, trumpeting: "diversification," "allocation of assets," "the 21st century will be the Asian century," "Russians will be giant capitalists."

You can add your own clichés. Most of them, unless you were very nimble, have been formulae for disaster. I find the only way to successfully invest outside your own country is either to have smart people living abroad advising you or to travel yourself, seeing the conditions and companies firsthand and making your own decisions.

And you must always mistrust certain buzz words like "the Asian tigers." The tigers have certainly turned into lambs in the last few years. As a matter of fact, when nicknames are given to any investment philosophy, like Asian tigers (they were the countries that "couldn't miss" for stock market profits—Malaysia, Thailand, Singapore, Indonesia, and so forth), it usually means that the game is almost over.

Almost everyone who reads this book went to college. Virtually every college class has a directory of classmates: what they do, where they live, etc. I always drop a note to classmates if I intend to visit their country, inviting them to dinner if we were friends, to have a drink if I didn't know them (people usually react positively to childhood and will be curious about you). And you should have faith in the fact that you will be interesting to them as well, even a treat for them if you have (and you should have) curiosity about the world.

I always ask my friends abroad, when I see them, "What are your favorite local companies that may be public?" And I always ask about politics and how the private economy may be doing. Because all foreigners are proud of their countries, too, I always get interesting, animated answers, which has led me to investigate companies as diverse as Volvo and Astra from Sweden (now Astra Zeneca), Novartis from Switzerland, South China Morning Post, Guinness (now Deago) from Great Britain, the Irish bank stocks, and many others with great worldwide names and strong liquidity for the American buyer.

I'll share with you some of my own experience with foreign investing. Years ago, my family disapproved mightily of a young lady about whom they thought I was much too serious. They figured the more they opposed the match, the more I'd pursue it. So they called in an expert on love, a Viennese banker married to an American heiress, to teach me about the proper conduct of affairs. My father thought that, though I ignored him, I'd pay attention to a European, experienced in the ways of the world.

With my father watching silently, the Viennese banker launched into his sermon. "Don't sell your destiny short by being so American. You are all so naïve," he told me, "so in a hurry to get everything organized in your lives. You miss all the flavor, the adventures. There are a thousand wonderful women from here to Vienna who were meant for you. There is no such thing as one person for one person. For instance," he added, "I have a niece. . . ."

The banker was portly, impeccably turned out, with suits from Saville Row and shirts from Jermyn Street, and an accent from somewhere along the Danube. How could I not yield to his European experience and sophistication?

I never married the young lady in question. But my family probably would have objected to Joan of Arc.

Years later, I realized that we as a nation are suffering from the same syndrome. Lured by the global sirens, American investors had poured money into foreign investments, believing the grass was much greener elsewhere.

Case in point. Lady Bancroft is a client of mine. I call her Lady Bancroft because she is an incurable Anglophile, even though she grew up outside Watertown, New York. She goes to the "chemists," not the drug store, for toothpaste, and to the "vintner's," not the liquor store, for single malt Scotch. Her favorite story involves her grandmother, who was English, and the advice she gave to Lady Bancroft's mother on her wedding night. The advice was simply this: "My dear, don't be surprised at anything that happens." You get the picture.

Several years ago, Lady Bancroft told me, "I want to invest in only foreign securities: the Far East, Great Britain, Europe. Don't put new money into anything American. America is like Rome before the fall; all the opportunities are elsewhere." I insisted she keep her old, low-cost list of U.S. companies, but henceforth, I agreed, she would buy only foreign stocks.

At her request, in the last several years, we bought stocks in Japan and Hong Kong which plummeted, Laura Ashley at $3 (now well under $1), and several individual country funds on the big board that have fallen as much as 70 percent from the purchase price. On the other hand, her old U.S. holdings—General Electric, Merck, Procter & Gamble, Exxon—have outperformed most indices.

In our yearend planning session, I pointed this out to her. She was outraged. "There is quality and service abroad," she insisted, "that we cannot get at home any longer. Anything foreign is preferable to anything American. Buy more of all of my foreign holdings!" I inquired as to the last time Lady Bancroft was abroad. "I have eyes," she responded. "I read; I go to travelogues. This is the decade of Europe. Buy more." First rule of survival: Take the order. So I retreated, with Lady Bancroft convinced that it was twilight in America.

With so many clients insisting on placing bets abroad, I knew it was time to pack my bags. So, shortly after, I went to London and had lunch with an old friend in the city who has a seat on the London Exchange. Cynicism has been Rodney's hallmark since childhood. He met me at a pub near the Exchange and insisted we have three gin and tonics apiece. "They're small, old boy, and the world is cruel."

At lunch, we had several carafes of wine. I told him about Lady Bancroft, and he laughed. "She wants England? Give her England—she'll be sorry," he said. "Nothing works here; foreigners own everything; prices are in the stratosphere, and we have lost control. We need a bulldog at the helm to feel good about ourselves—a Churchill, a Thatcher, a Duke of Wellington. Frankly, old sport," Rodney added, "I've been thinking of buying a little spread in Wyoming to have some freedom, some grandeur in my life, the kind you can only have in the American West."

He took me to another pub for an after-luncheon port, at which point he went back to work, and I was left to stagger around the city, looking at men in bowler hats carrying furled umbrellas, pondering the world's love–hate relationship with America.

I pursued this theme a week later, in Paris, with a client who slept most of the day, prowling the City of Light after dark. Josef came to France from Egypt as a young man. He never seemed to lack for money, having prospered in mysterious ways. His hobby was making the rounds of Parisian dives where he took the microphone and sang romantic American songs in English. "I want to be the French Sinatra," he told me. "No one in Paris sings 'Autumn Leaves' better than me. American TV, movies, and music are still the ultimate."

He's right about this theme, which is why I have profitably owned Viacom and Time Warner and Fox Entertainment. This is what the world wants from America, and if you buy the producers of this content, sooner or later you will thrive with these investments. It's common sense.

Josef promised to introduce me to a man who could explain the character of European investors to me. We found this man, Clark, an American expatriate educated in Switzerland, at the Ritz bar. In an earlier phase of his life, he had bought and sold companies on a grand scale, all over the world. Smoking unfiltered Camels and sipping brandy, he looked like the actor John Garfield. "Investing is simple," Clark told me. "I learned a lesson years ago: Every time I strayed from what I knew best, I got my tail handed to me.

"Let me tell you about the French. They are the world's greatest cynics. All they want to do is get money out of France because they don't trust their own government. They're terrified of having everything nationalized, taken away from them, although, with the euro, there are great signs for the first time that government is listening to free markets. The Rhone Poulenc Company alone has invested more than $3 billion in the United States in the past few years. And the French are violently anti-Japanese, but perversely, Japan is where they have invested the most."

He sipped his Cognac and continued. "Remember, unlike us, Europeans do not regard borders as important to investing. The Germans I know think Telefonica de Espana is a great buy. The Spanish think ELF Aquitane is a steal. And the British are mad about Fiat. Yet in America no one heard of investing abroad until a few years ago. Americans were so insular; even when they did invest overseas, they considered only a few familiar companies. They are viewed as children by the Europeans, with no wisdom of the Old World. But secretly they admire our openness and creativity, our ability to take risks.

"If I were to generalize," he went on, "I'd say the Anglo-Saxons want to keep their money in their own countries. The Latins desperately want their money anywhere but. And the Europeans are interested in real assets, not cash flow or potential earning power. They never even considered goodwill an investment factor until several years ago."

"How about the Swiss?" I asked. Clark smiled at me. "Do you know that the Swiss are lousy investors? All of my friends who have Swiss accounts complained for years about the performance of their portfolios. The Swiss hold onto your securities, convert all of your currencies into Swiss francs, and then charge you fat fees. They have one abiding passion: making money for their Swiss partners.

"I know Swiss bankers," he continued, "whose sole job it is to courier cash into London. The Brits arrange loans to the Swiss, but what they are really doing is loaning money to themselves—and the Swiss provide the documentation. European skiers in Gstaad all shop at Cartier and Boucheron, and only 5 percent of all turnover is by credit card. Every villa in Southern France is technically owned by some Swiss trust with the bank fronting them."

"All illegal?" I asked.

He winked at me. "What's legal? All I know is, it's the Swiss way—and I can use another spot of brandy."

On the flight home, I thought of a liberal journalist friend of mine. He wrote columns for many years full of scorn for things American. I remember him telling me about a trip he made to the Soviet Union, with VIP status all the way. "When I arrived back in New York," he told me, "I got down on my knees and kissed the tarmac, I was so glad to be home."

Investors in the new century, hot for the fad of foreign investing, should be sentenced to travel abroad, keeping their eyes wide open.

Investing Abroad—Part II

GIVEN A CHOICE OF SPEAKING WITH ECONOMISTS, global strategists from Wall Street, or street-smart people putting their own money on the line, I'll take street smarts every time. One of my good friends I call Sammy the Spread. He is one of the most focused people I have ever met, but he disguises this focus in jokes and smiles and bear hugs and in being totally disarming, like a big, jolly kid. Sammy the Spread looks like the classic banker, dressing in bespoke suits and shirts from Hilditch and Key of Jermyn Street.

Sammy is in the business of third-world debt, trying to figure out whose country's obligations (debts) he can buy at a discount and to whom he can sell these obligations at a premium. But anything that sounds simple, or looks simple from the outside, seldom is.

"You always say," Sammy said to me years ago, "that most of life happens by accident. Years ago, a neighbor of mine complained to me that a supplier to his business in Brazil owed him $25,000 and he couldn't get it back.

"I was a lawyer, and I told him maybe I could help, not telling him I had a classmate at law school from Rio de Janeiro. Over the phone with my classmate in Rio, I convinced him to see what he could do about collecting the debt. Of course, my classmate knew the supplier. In Latin America, most people doing big business know each other; many of them, in fact, are related. We got $15,000 for my neighbor, and I got 30 percent of that, $4,500 for one or two phone calls.

"Most collection agencies got 50 percent at the time, and many used strong-arm, intimidating methods. My happy neighbor put me in touch with his bank, which he knew had similar problems collecting on foreign debt. I told the bank I had many high-level connections abroad, and by God, they gave me $7 million worth of paper in Poland to collect. 'Fake it before you make it' became my motto," Sammy the Spread went on.

"Well," he said, "the bank fronted me the money to go to Poland, and the first thing I did was to go into Citibank in Warsaw and ask the assistant manager out for a drink, telling him that I may be bringing him a lot of business. Citibank owns foreign banking, so for a few vodkas I established a beachhead. In a couple of days, from other people, I learned the value of 'making the tip' in Poland, that everything was based on bribes: getting a plumber, installing a TV, reserving a table at a restaurant.

"It's a joke in the United States when you hear of American companies indicted for bribery abroad. Do you want to do business or not? America is really so parochial; it's like the typical U.S. headline in Boston is, 'Earthquake in Peru. Beacon Hill woman hurt.' Anyway, I also learned that the Poles, aside from drinking vodka, are very emotional, creative, and quite zany. So I was zany with the people who owed the $7 million, and I sold the loans to Citibank for $3.5 million, which then laid them off for $5 million when business improved in Poland and capitalism began to creep in. Everyone was happy, and my fee was around $250,000. Then I started to get into the listing books that documented foreign debt, and willy-nilly, I became an expert in a business that hadn't really ever formally existed. Fake it before you make it."

Sammy the Spread's gems of wisdom in foreign markets have been bled out to me over the years, and I thought I'd share the highlights with you:

1. In my business, once a country develops positive balance of payments, like Turkey in the early 1980s, it's time to move on. You can only make money in desperate situations (like the American bank stocks in '90–'91).

2. People love to talk. I fell into my profession by accident, and then I had nothing to lose. Ask a lot of questions. If you meet a seller of debt, ask, "Who else has called you?" for instance. Ask questions of your competitors and your clients. "Who's doing what to whom and for how much?" You'll be amazed what people tell you if you ask.

3. When you go to a third-world country, eat the same thing every meal. I've had great luck with tomato soup and spaghetti. Never try to eat gourmet in Lagos, for instance.

4. Remember this as a general observation: People are mostly good at making money but terrible at investing it.

5. In doing deals, you can generally trust the Germans, the Dutch, the English, and the Japanese, but only at the highest levels. The Russians are the worst, followed by the Nigerians, the Tanzanians, and the Zambians. The Russians have no sense of morality, even with letters of commitment. They won't even say, "Sorry," or give you an excuse for breaking a deal. The Colombians and Brazilians will at least say they're sorry after they screw you. Russia actually has done more damage to the West under their cowboy capitalism than during all the years of the cold war. But eventually, there is a lot of money to be made in Russia. Once you taste the joys of capitalism, there is no going back.

6. If you do not have your person or persons in place in each country, forget it. So often the analysts writing about emerging countries are all based in London. All over eastern Europe, the people carry little bags; everyone has one. In Hungary, they call them their "perhaps bags." *Perhaps* someone will fill them with money. If you're going to invest abroad, go local in your research—talk to locals who have their eyes open for their next opportunity. *Perhaps* this

method won't make you a lot of money, but it sure will save you a lot in the long run.

Sammy the Spread took me to lunch recently. He had the cuffs on his Grieves and Hawkes suit jacket folded back about 2 inches, revealing the real button holes unbuttoned on the cuffs.

"Nice touch," I said to him, pointing at his latest affectation of dress.

"What can I tell you," he says. "At least I look like a player. And give me a spread I can drive a truck through. I'll be a happy man."

Playing the Revolution

OF COURSE, WE'RE IN A REVOLUTION. Technology is transforming our lives daily. And many people seem threatened by it—the way, probably, they were threatened by the introduction of the automobile. Or television. None of us wants to feel redundant, and all of us want to make money in the market without feeling like a fool when prices go down.

New technologies, particularly those related to the Internet, are not cheap. The major players sell at prices reflecting potential growth far, far, into the future.

How can you participate with your head and not just your heart? You nibble. You buy a little America Online, a tad of eBay, a drop of Yahoo, and anything else that catches your fancy, no matter how pricey it appears to be. Then, after you've done your homework on your favorites, and you're convinced you're on the right track—that they have the potential to be one of the long-term winners in the market—you nibble a little more every time the price goes down 10 percent. This allows you to build a position in a smart way, buying odd amounts from a discount broker, or a full-service shop if they will accommodate you. Buy enough, in this "virtual savings plan" of your favorites—be it Microsoft, Cisco, Intel, or any of the others you feel will be the survivors—and over time, you will nibble your way to the top!

If this is too racy, I take the advice of a friend of mine, a professor at the Harvard Business School who likens the Internet frenzy to the gold rush in California in 1849. "None of the panners for gold made any money. The real winners were the people who sold picks and shovels to them."

So you buy the suppliers to Net users: AT&T, Lucent, even Staples, all who basically sell picks and shovels to Internet users . . . the supplies.

Doing It Yourself

I T'S AN AXIOM ABOUT THE LEGAL PROCESS, "THE person who represents himself in court has a fool for a client." I have done business with literally thousands of people over the course of my career. And not one of them, no matter how rich or how smart, was capable of managing his or her own money. A very small percentage could pick fine stocks; they even had a knack for spotting emerging trends, but they never knew how much to buy, or when to buy more if the stocks temporarily turned against them, or most important, when to sell. This is primarily because, as Adam Smith has said, quoting the first Mr. Johnson, the founder of Fidelity funds, "Investing is an art, not a science." You have to develop the feel for it. This can only come with time and experience.

I ask everyone who seeks to place money in my charge, "Do you want to make money or would you rather fool around?" It is a legitimate question because certain people will say, "You know, I've made my fortune, such as it is. Fooling around is exactly what I want to do. Money can be fun, you know."

Increasingly, Americans are trading the stock market for themselves. There is a whole generation of people who certainly want to make money. But in my opinion, they end up fooling around. I had George Brown in for lunch a few weeks ago. George is one of the pioneers of the discount brokerage business. You see his wonderful ads on CNBC and in the financial press. The ads feature George himself, a rumpled man, the kind you know would've been running a hardware or dry goods store 70 years ago, decent and hard working, someone for whom the business was everything. "Online," the ads say, "and broker trades for $5.00. An unattainable dream? Probably, unless you have watched your own money for at least five years and have $15,000 in cash or securities to open an account."

"Selling is in my blood," says George Brown, whose Brown and Company accounts for about 3 percent of the discount brokerage business. (Schwab represents some 40 percent of this trade.)

"We started in 1975," he told me, "just when negotiated commissions came in. We charged $25 plus 8 cents a share, virtually unheard of then. You had to have $40,000 net worth and five years experience in the market. Most of the new business came from California, the New World, so to speak. And it's corny, but people don't lie on forms. It's amazing what you can pick up about people."

Brown told me that his company processes some 12,000 trades a day through 12 offices. "Our customers know what they want," he said. "And what they want is that the cost of trading be cheap. We have full-service customers. Although at least 50 percent of them sooner or later leave to go back to full-service brokers when they discover how difficult it is to be hung out there all by themselves. How do we make money? We do it like the big guys, our profits came from the interest on the debit balances, the margin accounts. Most people don't know that interest charges are how brokerage firms make money, not from the commissions."

"What about your clientele?" I asked him.

"Our average account is around $180,000, more than 50 percent of the clients are over the age of 40, driving three cars, one for the kid in the house. But more and more younger people are trading with us online, online is now more than 30 percent of our business and growing. And more of this is going to come from overseas, worldwide trading."

George Brown seems to have the secret to long life: He loves what he does. "I have no real hobbies," he tells me. "The worst thing is to have purpose in life."

I laugh at his sense of irony. "You probably went to Harvard."

He allows himself a small smile. "Class of '49," he tells me.

"I'll bet you have a favorite quote or phrase."

"It's from Emerson. 'Consistency is the hobgoblin of small minds.' I'll never retire, though. Retirement is death. My father is a lawyer and an accountant, and he comes to work every day; he's 96."

I ask Brown about young people today, and he tells me, "very smart but much less tolerant than earlier generations. I resent their leaving, job hopping after we've trained them. They are much more sure of themselves than we were but . . ." he pauses, "they haven't really been tested yet. They will be, of course."

I asked him finally about his own style of investing. "I'm like the owners of the casino. I get my piece either way. I do not enjoy investing myself. I let others do it for me. I like sure things. And I can't wait to get into the office every day."

"Any words about success in life?" I asked him.

"Sure," George Brown said to me. "Always keep success in perspective. My mother helps with that. She says, 'You turned out great, George. But you're no Charles Schwab.'" He was too excited to hang out with me for long; he couldn't wait to get back to the business.

Individual trading, as opposed to trades by institutions, has mushroomed with the growth of online ability to do it yourself. Even Merrill Lynch is joining this revolution announcing a move to allow their clients to trade online.

People have traded various markets by themselves for thousands of years, from silks and spices in China to the Internet stocks today. Let me tell you about several do-it-yourselfers in my experience and where I think it leads.

In the good old days before negotiated commissions (pre-1975), clients would sit around in the boardroom of brokerage offices, watching the ticker tape, keeping warm, being social. Brokerage firm boardrooms were little clubs with their own pecking orders. Clients would take the same seats every day, being superstitious about their "lucky" locations. A handful of these boardroom regulars claimed that trading the market was how they made their living.

Large Larry Viser was one of these people. Large Larry looked almost exactly like the character actor Cesar Romero, with thick, silver hair swept back like a Roman senator, a perpetually tan face in the middle of which a large cigar seemed permanently stuck. Large Larry wore a diamond ring on his right pinky, Italian-cut suits with highly polished Italian pointy shoes and silk socks with little geometric figures on them, and of course, Countess Mara ties, many times lavender or even white, as if he were always going to walk out of the boardroom and go directly to central casting for a George Raft movie of the 1940s.

"Kid," he'd say to me, "I live by my wits. But I intend to be farting through silk until I die. Buy me 1,000 Aideback Oil at $8." Large Larry came in every day and traded the market, grabbing a point here, two points there, always on margin to the maximum allowable. Large Larry also had a DVP account. This meant "delivery versus payment." The stock he bought would be delivered out to a bank for safekeeping. And the bank would pay for the trade.

Actually this process involved Larry borrowing money from a "factor," a money lender who, for exorbitant interest rates would loan Large Larry money to leverage himself even higher than brokerage firms would allow. Larry would sit and trade, hocked up to his silver eyebrows, smoke his cigars, knock the ashes into his paper cup of coffee (which he would drink from sometimes when he was really excited about the market), and claim he was making a big living.

That was in bull markets. In bear markets, he would disappear for months at a time. We would get calls from banks, insurance companies, people who gave him car loans, and landlords hunting him down. Then he would surface as if nothing had happened, kick someone out of his chair, and trade again; 1,000 this, 5,000 that, ride the momentum, and exit. On one of these re-entries, I noticed the diamond pinky ring was gone. "Last piece of the puzzle, my boy," he said, imitating W. C. Fields. "Last piece of the puzzle." This usually meant it was at a pawn shop or given up to a loan shark somewhere near the airport where a few broken bones in the pursuit of debts is not a big deal.

"Do you expect to get rich from trading?" I asked Large Larry after he had reappeared in our lives once again. It was a June day, and I was walking him to his car, a black Cadillac Fleetwood with black upholstery. He retrieved the car from the doorman at the hotel where Larry always parked, palmed the doorman a five, and slid in. "I expect my trading to keep me going," he said, "to buy the cigars, duke the doorman and the maitre d'. Trading gives me down payments," he said. "That's all I need. Down payments." Large Larry never left rubber when he left the scene. And he died broke.

"Are you serious?" Louis the Kid asked me as if he thought I were nuts. "Of course, I do it to get rich." This is the trader of today. Louis the Kid is 28 years old, majored in computer science at Babson College, has not worn a tie since his sister's wedding five years ago, and currently has no regular job with health benefits and a 401K plan. His father is a client of mine, and Louis thinks his dad is an idiot to do business with me when he could be piggybacking on Louis's success, day trading his way to financial security.

"I started with 25 grand," Louis the Kid told me when his father first brought him to my office. "I basically tapped my rollover from my first job, figured I'd pay the taxes, and I'd probably make what I paid out, in the first week of trading. It took me a week and a half, actually, in and out of Intel, three times that last day." Louis's father told me his son had made $125,000 the previous year, day trading on the Internet.

"Louis was always great with numbers," his father told me. "I've given him some money to play with, and my friends are pushing to give him money also. After all, didn't George Soros basically start this way?"

Louis was dressed in jeans, polo shirt, and red high-top Converse All-Star sneakers. He was chewing Double Bubble gum, popping bubbles, then starting over. He could not sit down, wandering my office, playing with objects scattered about, in motion constantly, and jabbering while he moved. "I don't ever need a job in the traditional sense," he said. "Why would you if your antennae are out and you can live by your wits? I've got a few toys, a B-mer, an old Indian bike, a condo on the water. I don't have time for relationships, or marriage. The screen is the scene," he said. "I'm totally in there, on margin, half a point here, three quarters there, in and out. This year I'll make 200 grand, easy."

There are supposedly over five million of these like-minded day traders going online, paying virtually no commissions and trading literally millions of shares daily, especially in small cap Internet stocks whose values are affected enormously by the constant turnover created by this new breed of speculator, who meet in cyberspace, in chat rooms, and who jump in and out of stocks, sometimes dozens of times a day.

It would be easy to despise Louis the Kid: cocky, positive that he had "the way," contemptuous of anyone in the money game who was at all traditional. But I loved his energy, his optimism, which I thought would stand him in good stead when he eventually went broke. For go broke Louis the Kid inevitably will, even though his costs of trading are pennies per share, and forgetting that his short-term trades are penalized at the highest tax rate. (He'll probably pay 35 to 40 percent tax on all of his profits.)

Sometimes in life, particularly with our children, you can see and understand everything. But you cannot do a damn thing about it. People have to make their own mistakes, be hammered in life at various times and learn by it. Or not, as the case may be. I took Louis the Kid and his father down the elevator and across the lobby and on to the garage below the building. Louis walked ahead of us to the garage elevators. Bopping was more like it. He bounced as he walked in his high-tops, knowing deep down that he could day trade his way into the Investing Hall of Fame.

"He really seems to have it," his father said to me. "Maybe he's actually found the formulae. I've given him money to trade. And he's way up so far. It's a lot less boring, you have to admit, than the AT&T and GTE you've got me in." Ahhhh, how quickly they forget, I thought, with both those stocks trading near all-time highs, not counting the dividend streams. Petty of me, I know.

In the garage, Louis the Kid said to me, "Nice building. But the rent, the insurance, the support staff. I do it all myself. I don't even need an office. 'Why Don't We Do It in The Road?'" he sang from the Beatles song. Louis gave me a thumbs down as he peeled by me in his BMW. His dad flashed me a sheepish grin and shrugged as he sat in the passenger seat, a redundant dad with his kid for the millennium.

I had an image of good ol' Large Larry Viser, sliding away in his Cadillac Fleetwood, knowing that he, too, could trade himself into the Hall of Fame. As F. Scott Fitzgerald would say, "So we beat on, boats against the current."

RESEARCH

AND

DEVELOPMENT

Grabbing for the Leprechaun's Coat

SOME YEARS AGO, I WAS IN A RESORT HOTEL WITH several hundred other money managers and stockbrokers. It was a black-tie affair—a Saturday night after a day of golf, tennis, and beach, where rewards for producing fees or commissions at the highest level of the firm would be bestowed. Our big treat after dinner was to listen to the featured speaker of the weekend, Alan Greenspan; this was before he became head of the Federal Reserve Board. Mr. Greenspan spoke for about 45 minutes. Luckily, most of the people in the room were three sheets to the wind, and talking with their tablemates, because Greenspan was almost completely unintelligible in return for his extraordinary retainer. After the speech, there was to be a question-and-answer session.

"Aha," say I, and shot my arm into the air. "Two specific questions, Mr. Greenspan," I said. "Remember, this is a roomful of stockbrokers who love instant gratification. My first question is: Do you personally own stocks?

Second question: If you do not own stocks but wanted to, what kinds of companies would you buy?" Pretty straightforward, right? He wandered on for 15 more minutes, about money supply, consumer price index, trade imbalance, and never answered either question. One broker from Lehman Brothers yelled out from the back of the room, "Can the band play 'New York, New York'?" And the economist retreated to our chairman's table. Our chairman took down the name of the broker.

The next day, my wife and I were flying in a puddle jumper to Miami on the way home. Two seats in front of us on the small plane was Greenspan. I said to my wife, "He can't get away from me now. I'm going to get 'the word.'" She tried to restrain me, but I got up and squatted right down in the aisle next to the great man. Greenspan was buried in paperwork, which he tried to cover up as I knelt next to him. Was he covering up the formula to riches beyond my wildest dreams?

"I know you couldn't give 'the word' to all those greedy stockbrokers," I said. "I don't blame you. Pearls before swine and all that," I added. "But we're almost alone now. Would you be buying stocks, and if so, which ones?"

He peeked at me over his glasses. "I'm trying to work," he said.

"Does that mean you wouldn't be buying stocks? You know I fell in love with *The Fountainhead* in college." I knew Greenspan had been close to Ayn Rand and her objectivist movement. How could he resist this approach?

"I'm trying to work," he repeated and rattled his paperwork, but still holding it away from my gaze. Stonewalling me. I could stay squatting in the aisle, or I could retreat. The plane began to bump, and the seatbelt light flicked on. "Ayn Rand wouldn't approve of stonewalling me." I had the last word.

"Are we rich yet?" My wife asked as I sat down and buckled up.

"I think he was trying to tell me to put all of my money in Treasury bills and hold out for big speaking fees."

"The emperor's new clothes," she said, and opened up the latest James Lee Burke mystery.

This may sound like a lesson in obscurity, but it points up a principle that is key in managing money. If anyone proposes to watch over your funds, be it investment advisor, financial planner, or stockbroker, ask him or her two questions.

What is your personal investment philosophy?
What kinds of securities do you own for yourself?

You can take this a little further and ask what his or her biggest success has been. And what has been his or her biggest failure? If the investment advisor, financial planner, or stockbroker cannot articulate his or her philosophy in a few simple paragraphs, find someone else to watch over your money. There is an old line, "Them that can't do, teach." It may be okay in golf or at business schools, but for hands-on money management, go with someone who's been in the wars, and won.

Who Are "They"?

ALL TOO OFTEN, PEOPLE SAY SOMETHING ALONG the lines of, "*They* say that high technology stocks are the only place to be," or "*They* say that inflation is heating up and that interest rates are going to rise." Who are "they"? CNBC is now watched daily by millions of Americans. Little TVs have even invaded brokerage offices. Recently, we were given the choice of having cable hooked into every individual office so that we would know presumably what was really going on.

"What do we pay millions of dollars to our research department for?" I ask in vain.

"Well," I am told, "they have all these experts all day long on the TV."

"If you think like a tourist," I say, "you'll always be a tourist; you'll never learn how to belong."

"If you have the flu," I tell people, "and you sit in bed and watch CNBC all day, I believe you'll feel like selling all of your stocks and bonds and then slitting your wrists. All these experts, all this jargon, all these predictions."

We are on information overload today; it is impossible to sift through it all. There was a market strategist who got quite famous because of television; he predicted the crash of 1987 several weeks before it happened. This right guess was milked for all it was worth, and the strategist was given a fund to run. That adventure proved to be a disaster. The strategist could strategize but couldn't pick stocks or manage money. "Those that can't do, teach," goes the saying, and like many sayings, there's a reason for them. The strategist was subsequently fired, but he continues to thrive today, still making predictions and focusing on self-marketing efforts based on that one great stock market call years ago. This is the ploy often mentioned by market letter writer Raymond DeVoe in one of his many useful rules, "If you've ever been right in your life, never let them forget it."

Further comments on the art of prediction: The best story about interest rates I've ever heard is from my friend Eric, a corporate lawyer specializing in international mergers and acquisitions. "One of my clients is one of America's premier venture capitalists," Eric told me. "He had a meeting recently in the main dining room of one of New York's biggest banks. There were seven other people at the meeting; four Fortune 500 CEOs, two senior officers of the bank, and the president of an investment banking firm. My friend has a rather large ego, always trying to upstage everyone else. The meeting is underway. The executives are all discussing the direction of interest rates for the next six months. My friend pulls out his cell phone. He dials his office right in the middle of the meeting. The other executives are furious that he would be so rude, especially when they hear him say to his secretary, 'Ms. Russell, any messages for me? Uh huh, uh huh, uh huh.' As the others get even angrier, my friend says, 'By the way, Ms. Russell, where do you think interest rates are going to be six months from now? Uh huh, uh huh.'"

"My friend hung up the phone and looked across the table at stony silence. He smiled at the assembled men. 'Ms. Russell,' he said, 'says that she has no idea where interest rates are going to be in six months.' He paused. 'And neither do any of you assholes.'"

Be skeptical about what "they" predict. Don't take as gospel everything you hear on television from "experts." Have you ever met anyone who is on television? Or comments on radio? Or writes for newspapers? Are they the smartest people you know about money matters?

Asking the Right Questions

I AM STRIVING CONSTANTLY TO SIMPLIFY MY LIFE and the lives of my clients wherever possible. Years ago I joined a golf club and, on my first day as a member, I toured the facilities, ending up in the locker room. Poking around by myself, an attendant stopped me and asked if he could help me find something. I introduced myself, shook his hand and, since he had a recognizable brogue, I said, "Where did you grow up?"

"Ireland," he smiled.

"Wouldn't be anywhere near Galway?" I guessed.

He beamed at me and we chatted for a while and I even sang him a few bars of a song I had heard there. He went on about home and his family and then suddenly said, "I'm sorry, I'm probably keeping you from golf."

"And you'd be doing a favor to the golf course," I said, which cracked him up. The next time I came, Tim the attendant gave me the best locker space (I thought) at the club and the best attention to anything I or my guests could want.

The question, "Where did you grow up?" is so simple and basic, yet seldom do you hear people ask it. It helps, of course, if you care about people who pass through your life.

I also often ask people, "What were you like in high school?" The usual reaction is one of delight. We all love to talk about ourselves, and childhood particularly brings unusual responses from people. But the process brings a form of instant intimacy, and if you're seeking information from anyone about virtually anything, you will find out a lot more of what you're seeking.

Asking the right question is also the key to your "commonsense" research. Here's an example. A stock I had owned over the years, and always prospered with, had been Tampax, which, through a name change, became Tambrands. You can no longer buy the stock because, in 1997, they were taken over by Procter & Gamble.

But here were my thought processes *before* I bought the shares. Tampax was dominant in their field of feminine hygiene, tops in quality and reliability. Several years ago, they had management problems, and the stock dropped from the $60s to the mid-30s. The great name recognition was still there, however. And the quality. In my experience, with the companies that become suddenly unloved, like AT&T, or IBM, or American Express, companies that were vilified for a time, a catalyst in the form of new management often comes in and changes the perception of stocks that Wall Street loves to hate. I thought Tambrands would be one of these overlooked values, and aside from exploring company reports, I began buying the stock for two reasons. The first reason was demographics. Most of the world was, and is, fairly primitive in relation to the United States. Introduction of any feminine hygiene methods into China, India, Latin America, or Africa would someday probably be a big plus for Tampax. And I'm patient. I can afford to wait for an obvious idea to kick in.

The second reason I bought the stock was the response I got to some research that anyone can do—ask the user of products. I had one of my female assistants ask all of our female office employees (65 of them):

1. What feminine protection they used.
2. Did price matter to them in choosing this product?
3. Are they loyal to the brand?

Seventy percent of the women used Tampax tampons. Most of the women were not price sensitive on this issue. And also, most tended to remain with what they felt was the quality brand.

Asking the right questions is often your best research.

Ask the unusual question and you'll be rewarded with unusual answers. The process might even make your relationships a lot better.

Market Research in Your Neighborhood

I BELIEVE THAT THE MORE YOU CAN PERSONALIZE your life, the better service and information you can obtain. Whenever I shop, I ask the sales help how business is, what's selling, what are the most popular brands. My local druggist tells me everything, from which painkillers are moving, to inquiries about impotence drugs from male customers, to the favorite condom brand (usually Trojans, made by Carter Wallace, which trades on the New York Stock Exchange).

Most good druggists or grocers are "schmoozers"; they love to talk to the customers, and they live to gossip. I have to listen to Harry, my druggist, tell me about who he thinks is sleeping with whom in the neighborhood. "I did a survey of all the guys who came in here recently," Harry tells me, "and asked them if they think oral sex with a woman not your wife is cheating. Every man said it wasn't really cheating, that only intercourse constituted infidelity."

Harry smiled. "Then I asked all my women customers. Guess what? Every one of them said they would be on to their lawyers in a New York minute if even a whiff of oral sex were in the air. As it were."

Harry has one of those small, old-fashioned drugstores, probably as long as your living and dining room put together, but with thousands of items stacked from the ceiling to the floor, everything you might need from extra fine ballpoint pens to Gold Bond powder. And Harry knows what everyone needs, before they need it. "Pfizer's new drug for impotence," he tells me, "is going to be huge." I owned the stock, really, because of Harry.

Often, the most effective research on a company I receive is right around the corner from my house, at the neighborhood drugstore or grocery. I realize that in the large cities of America these "personal" places still exist. But in most of the country, you fill your drug prescriptions and buy your food in the chains—CVS or Osco, Stop & Shop or Vons, or some other superstore.

Every community probably has a 7-11 store or similar all-purpose enterprise. Even though personnel turnover is high, there is usually a bright, young employee who is paying attention to what's happening in the store, someone who "gets it," someone ambitious—who is probably going to move on sooner rather than later.

I always ask the employees, "Anything unusual selling here? Anything that you think is amazing, any product that is flying off the shelves? What soft drink moves the best?" If you ask enough questions, you get answers. The young people who do get it start to really pay attention, take notes, and have thanked me for teaching them new ways to look at life and consumer patterns.

Trust Your Instincts—but Do Your Homework

I STRONGLY BELIEVE IN EYES-AND-EARS INVESTING, as popularized by Peter Lynch. And I would much rather do my own research on companies, independent from what management of the companies (if you can talk with them) tell you.

Most often, CEOs of public companies are cheerleaders for their own regimes. They want to tell you optimistic news because they desperately want their predictions to come true. Many of my biggest mistakes have come from being too close to management. Most of what CEOs have told me over the years represented wishful thinking on their part. Once, a president of a direct-mail company told me, "We're going to be a $100 stock." The company was selling for $8. He was offended when I said to him, "I'd settle for $20."

"You've got no vision, son," he said. "That's why you're a stockbroker and I run my own business." I went to the parking lot after seeing the president, and pulling in next to my car were two employees in a company station wagon. "I manage people's money," I said to them. "And I'm thinking about buying stock in your corporation. How do you like working here?"

The first employee said, "They treat us like mushrooms in this company."

"Yeah," said the second employee, "kept in the dark and covered with shit."

"Management grabs with both hands," added the first. "Not much trickles down to us. I'd sell it short if I were you."

Often you tend to get misinformation from both management and employees. The boss is only optimistic. The workers see only the warts. Same company, but often wildly dissimilar observations.

When I get a chance to talk to management, I always seek out an employee or two to see the other side of the coin. It helps me make a better evaluation of investment possibilities.

Have you noticed articles in magazines and newspapers in the last several years about the so-called paperless society? Like world peace and loving your neighbor, this is a dream that is probably unreachable. When I was talking to a thoughtful friend about this subject, he said to me, "Do you know about Iron Mountain?"

"Is it a novel by Thomas Mann?" I asked.

He looked down his nose at me. "It's the largest records management storage business in America." Iron Mountain is indeed that, with revenues exceeding $400 million a year.

I came back from lunch with my friend that day and found an intern in my office sitting at a desk surrounded by annual reports stacked so high they almost obscured him from view. "What the hell is this?" I asked my crew.

"Oh, a new rule," they said. "Any company we invest in, we have to keep the annual reports on file for five years."

"That's ridiculous," I said. They shrugged, used to my railings against bureaucracy. But go to any law firm or corporate office or hospital. They are drowning in paper. So much of this volume has to be saved for X number of years, a requirement of the IRS and other government agencies. Iron Mountain fills an extraordinary need in today's society. Companies and individuals have their files and documents picked up by the storage company, and they pay rent every month while the paper continues to mount. What about microfilming everything? This solution is years away from being practical. Meanwhile, Iron Mountain continues to buy up storage companies around the country, and abroad, growing by acquisition, installing its systems, and quietly building an empire.

I would see the Iron Mountain trucks on the streets of my city. Several times I stopped to talk with the drivers. "How long have you worked for the company?" I asked them. "How do they treat their employees?" In all cases, I got wonderful reports about the decency of management and the hard-working ethic they fostered. The trucks were always spotlessly clean as well, as contrasted with one of their competitors. (I do like to invest in companies where there seems to be pride reflected in what they do.) I bought the stock mostly in the low teens. It now sells at $30. The reasons I bought it originally are just as compelling today.

This example shows how important it is for you to watch for society-wide trends to develop into new investment opportunities—and how it's equally important to do your own research in checking them out.

The Box King

ANYONE WHO MANAGES OTHER PEOPLE'S money, or anyone who invests for himself or herself, should have a box king in his or her life. I have a box king named Herbie. Herbie is on his fourth marriage. He gives each wife the nickname of a town in which he has gambled. He calls his current wife Vegas because it's his favorite gambling town. The other three wives, in descending order, he calls, San Juan, Atlantic City, and Tahoe. Herbie is my client, and he has a very good eye for companies that should thrive in the future. But better than that, Herbie's business can almost infallibly predict the direction of interest rates over a one- or two-year period.

Herbie manufactures boxes. And all of his customers ship their goods in Herbie's boxes. His customers include manufacturers of all kinds, from computer makers, to machine tool manufacturers, to retailers of all sorts. His clientele is extremely broad based and really mirrors society as a whole.

Every three months, I call Herbie and ask him, "How's business?" When Herbie tells me, "I'm flat out. We're on double shifts, six days a week, and I can't keep up with it," I know that five or six months down the line, interest rates are going to move up and the stock market will be in trouble. (Stock markets hate higher interest rates.) Conversely, when he tells me, "I haven't seen business this bad in ages. Everyone is complaining. Our biggest competitor is down to four days a week, and liner board prices are plunging." (Liner board is the primary ingredient for boxes.) That's when I buy bonds heavily, for sure as spring used to mean the circus was coming, when Herbie's business turns soft, five or six months down the road, interest rates are declining. The corrugated box business is a leading economic indicator, one that I find invaluable.

Chances are, there is a box king in or near your town. In some cases, you can be honest about it, call the boss and ask him (or her) yourself, "How's business?" Or you can ask your friends if they know a box manufacturer. As market predictors, they're a lot more reliable than economists. And, at least with Herbie, my box king, they're a lot more fun. When the box business is bad, buy bonds. When it's hot, sell them.

You Need a Net
Youngblood in
Your Life

I BELIEVE THAT, IN LIVING THE SMART LIFE, YOU always need something to trade. In our increasingly anonymous society of voice mails and 1-800 numbers, I find people are longing for the human touch, personal advice, and counsel. Most of you have hobbies and interests outside of your profession. This expertise and passion can be traded for services that you need. Simple examples: I got an appointment with a difficult-to-reach ophthalmologist in exchange for a promise of the best reading list he's had in years. A friend of mine obtained Super Bowl tickets by offering several free fly fishing lessons in exchange. Today, almost all of us could use help from a youngblood who is proficient in surfing the Net and can teach us about the new world of cyberspace. We're in a revolution—and young people are as comfortable in it as we were in white bucks and poodle skirts long ago.

The best way to recruit your Net youngblood is from within your own family. I'm sure all of you have a child, a niece or nephew, or a grandkid who is deeply into the Net. Take them for a special dinner, a game of tennis or golf, a hike. And have you tell them stories of what you can do on the Internet, the way, perhaps, you told *them* stories when they were *really* little. Thank goodness I can do this with my children. But I had a youngblood from outside the family, a senior at a local college, majoring in computer science, in to see me last week. Her mother is a client and asked if I would give her a career counseling session. "Sure, if I can pick her brain, also," I said.

She knows me. "Don't give her any foolish ideas," she warned. A week later, in came Jane the Youngblood, eager to be out in the world. After listening to me talk about life after college, she launched into her tales of the Web. "It's perfect for us," Jane said. "Our generation does not believe in deferred gratification. We want it all *now*. *Time* is the biggest part of the Internet revolution. Think about it," she says. "My father used to take me to the library at night for school projects. I'd have to wait for him to take me home. Now I visit *ten* libraries on the Net and have to wait for no one."

"It's like the wild west, it seems to me," I said. "Totally out of control."

"Sure," this wise student told me. "And the Net is changing every day. It used to be about the number of eyeballs clicking on a Web page. Now it's 'what are you selling?' It's about building brands. People want to be comfortable when they go to a site, like trusting Coke, or McDonald's. Branding—or adding value. Our generation is also big on freedom. Don't work for anyone else, start your own business. And the real first rule of the Net is, it's the ultimate democracy."

Jane went on to agree with me that we all need a youngblood in our lives. "The average college student is online up to four hours a day. You have no fear when you're young. It's like, if you take up skiing at forty, you tend to ease your way down the slope. At ten it's "bang, crash, get out of the way." For us, the Net is a giant puzzle, and we compare notes constantly. We explore. It's like when you were a kid, probably, going into the woods to play with frogs, skip stones on a pond…not scared at all. But on the Net, ultimately, you better give the customers what they want."

I was full of wonder at everything Jane told me. "What can I teach you?" I asked.

She smiled. "I hope you can tell me what I'm missing, maybe about how one stays married for a long time, maybe how I learn from my mistakes…"

A wise child, my Net youngblood. Find something you can trade to have one (or more) in your life.

WHOM

CAN YOU

TRUST?

Five Questions to Ask
Your Broker

SOME TIME AGO, THERE WAS AN ARTICLE ABOUT Merrill Lynch suing Oppenheimer & Company for Oppenheimer's alleged stealing of Merrill Lynch clients. Few people outside the investment business I spoke with really understood this story. Several clients thought it was more tales of investment firms playing fast and loose with the customers' monies. The Merrill Lynch suit sought to stop the practice of other firms recruiting Merrill brokers by paying up-front bonuses and many other perks. Who owns the clients anyway? Is my brother-in-law my firm's client if I leave? Is he my client? Rodney Dangerfield would say, "Take my brother-in-law, please." Or is it mother-in-law?

Merrill Lynch was for a while the only Wall Street firm that played hardball with defecting brokers. They believe (after spending around $200,000 to train a brokerage rookie) that they own the clients. They will litigate to protect their interpretation of investment relationships. Most other firms move them in and move them out, realistically understanding the footloose nature of Wall Street personnel.

I happen to admire Merrill Lynch as a business. Every time the stock market tanks, and no one wants brokerage stocks, I will put Merrill high on my buy list. (Last summer, for instance, Merrill went from $90 to as low as $36. I bought for some clients at $45. The stock now stands, less than a year later, at $75.)

Recently, a long winter had just ended, and my car was covered with that relentless corrosive crust of salt. My wife and I lined up at a downtown car wash entrance. As we turned in, a car came out of a side ramp, straight for us, its horn blowing frantically. I was stuck between two cars and couldn't move, and the driver of the other car knew that I was stuck. He kept leaning on the horn, and then he leapt out of the driver's seat. I reached for my door handle, heart pumping furiously. My wife grabbed my arm. "Don't get out. That guy's crazy. Probably got an Uzi under the seat."

"Move the car," the man yelled. Then he laughed, and I realized it was someone I had worked with long ago, George the Gunner. I rolled down my window. "Just didn't want you to have a relaxed Sunday," he said. "What's life without the old adrenaline jumping?"

"I ought to punch you in the snoot," I said.

"You still can't take a joke," George snorted at me. "Uptight is no way to go through life, son."

We parted, but I thought about him.

The Merrill Lynch versus Oppenheimer suit is tailor-made to George's experience, so I called him about it.

"Lincoln freed the slaves," George said to me. "Stockbrokers are individual entrepreneurs as far as I'm concerned." George the Gunner has made almost as much of a living from hopping between brokerage firms as he has from servicing clients. He has worked for 8 different companies in 15 years, taking a healthy check each time—a bonus for signing—if you will. Here's how the typical deal works: George is contacted by a head-hunting firm or directly by a branch manager or sales manager of a brokerage house.

I know personally that many times the chairman or the president of a stock exchange firm will call to recruit a broker. "What do we have to do to get you to our shop?" they will ask. Most deals will pay the defecting broker up to 100 percent of the prior year's gross commissions, parceled out as 50 percent cash and 50 percent at a higher commission rate than normal for a specified period. But there are endless variations on this theme.

A recent situation I have seen involved a broker who did $2 million in gross commissions last year. He was paid $1.2 million up-front cash—and would get 50 percent of whatever he produced the next year. Not as good as a wide receiver would get. But not borscht, either. The big producers can hold out for stronger transition packages (50 percent of commissions for three years instead of one, for example).

Special perks can be layered on top of the purely monetary considerations. After all, ego plays a big role in these deals, and all big producers are really little boys and little girls at heart. Expense accounts and garage parking are no-brainers. George the Gunner has negotiated such perks as a three-year lease on his BMW, his country club dues, a skiing vacation in Switzerland, and his new office painted yellow (a power color at the time), along with a view up the Charles River so he could tell clients he went to Harvard. (He didn't.)

George is called Gunner because he shoots from the hip, a charming hustler whose line of chatter is portable in the increasingly gypsylike atmosphere of the modern investment business. At one point in his career, George was sued for unprofessional conduct. He had been sleeping with one of his clients at the office. The client followed him, however, on one of his periodic job hops, and had sex with him at his next firm as well.

During the arbitration surrounding the suit, the two investment houses insisted that they pay damages only in proportion to the number of times George had slept with his client at each firm. If he had sex twice as often at firm B as he had at firm A, then firm B had to pay the plaintiff twice as much. The wisdom of Solomon.

Of course, George could sell, which after all is the point in a sales-driven organization. How good a salesman is he? Once, a young client came to him in tears. "You've lost all my money," she cried. "I don't even have enough left to feed my horses."

Without skipping a beat, George the Gunner said, "Look, I know we've missed a few. But I think it's fate—karma—that you came in today and mentioned horses. There is a little cash left in your account, and I have a fantastic opportunity—Pinto Petroleum. Can't you see? We can get it all back. Karma!"

As I have written, this is a business that is driven by fear and greed. George the Gunner will always be around. He is good at making people greedy. But if fooling around is not your aim, here's how to hire the right guide.

If possible, meet your prospective broker or money manager face to face. It's the old prisoner-of-war drill: When you make personal contact with people, it makes it much more difficult for them to ignore you, persecute you, or treat you badly. Wherever possible in life, personalize your relationships. This applies to your dealings with lawyers and doctors as well. Any relationship you can make more personal improves your chances of success.

Furthermore, try to do business with someone who has a classic type A, obsessive-compulsive personality. These people need to be adored (or at least needed). Because of this, they tend to kill you with service and attention. They really want your portfolio to work—because of their ego, not yours.

And since what you all really want is not action but a plan to set you free financially, here are some questions to ask anyone who presumes to handle your money.

1. *Do you know anything about history, art, or literature?* It is my personal prejudice that anyone who watches my money should know a lot about the past, about human nature. Good money management is more about understanding emotion than it is about quantitative analysis. Your money manager should be working with both sides of his or her brain.

2. *What is your philosophy of investing?* Make sure that whoever is going to watch your nest egg can articulate what he or she believes in—in simple sentences. If you cannot explain to your stupidest relative what your broker or investment advisor believes in, you shouldn't be investing with that person.

3. *Do you own stock yourself?* (You'd be amazed how many financial consultants own no securities themselves.) Ask what the broker or investment advisor currently owns and what he or she has learned from successes and failures.

It's *Your* Money

ARE YOU THE KIND OF PERSON WHO WOULD, IF jostled in a theater lobby by someone rude, say, "Excuse me," when it's not your fault?

I believe that you should be a squeaky wheel, that you should be a strong advocate with your doctors, lawyers, and especially with your money managers. I have several clients who also have money with a hedge fund manager. They cannot read their statements, which seem to be purposefully incoherent. My clients are reluctant to ask for explanations, not wanting to seem unsophisticated. I say that if someone who wants to manage your money cannot explain his or her philosophy in a simple paragraph, then you shouldn't let him or her manage that money. And if those who do manage your money cannot simply explain their own statements to you, then you are probably headed for a sad experience.

It's *your* money; always remember that. Money managers tend to think that, once the funds are deposited, it's their money—and the clients are nothing more than an annoyance. Cure them of this notion. Call them once a month to see what's happening, and when you do, have an idea ready for your manager or broker. Tell him or her, "I hear the new Gillette razor is phenomenal," or, "I'm playing Calloway clubs, and I think the stock is cheap." Make your money manager give you an intelligent response, so you will stick in his or her brain as a person who is part of the process—not just a customer.

I tell new clients that my best ideas come from them, from their interaction with the world—and that I want them to check in with me if they have any bright ideas about companies, products, or services they enjoy. I also tell them to call me once a month, even if markets are stable and everything is fine in our financial lives. If they call me once a month, I can be up to date on what concerns them, and they can know about my thoughts of the moment.

Get Your Signals Straight

A WOMAN CAME TO ME SEVERAL YEARS AGO AND told me, "I deal in old prints and drawings, and I'm moving to London shortly. Here's a check for $300,000. I want income and safety out of this. Income, income, income. Because I don't know if I can make a living out of what has been a hobby, meaning prints and drawings."

"You want income and safety of your principal, right?" I said.

"Right," she answered. She left me the check and went off to London. I invested her money strictly for income, as she insisted: corporate bonds, preferred stocks, some tax-free municipal bonds, and assorted U.S. Treasury issues, setting the account up so that she could write herself a check once a month. This was in June 1996. At the end of the year, I received a fax from her. "I see that the market has been hot, not much progress in my account. What's happening?" I faxed her back. "You're invested for income, income, income. Happy New Year."

Halfway through 1997, she faxed me again. "Market still hot. How am I doing versus the Standard & Poors 500 average?" This is somewhat like saying on the golf course after shooting 103, "How am I doing compared with Tiger Woods?" Or more precisely, "How am I doing compared to people playing tennis?"

"This is not what you're doing," I faxed her. "Your money is designed to move sideways and throw off the income you need to live on." After a few days, I received another fax. "Transferring account to Merrill Lynch."

Fear and greed, of course. It's what makes the investment business run. And it's fine to change the rules in the middle of the game because it's *your* money. But you should learn something about yourself as part of the process, and it's amazing how many people never do. When you begin having your money managed, write down your goals *before* you get started. Here are a few of the most important questions to ask yourself:

1. Am I invested for growth or income?
2. Do I want a combination of these goals?
3. How high is my tolerance for risk?
4. Has the advisor made his or her philosophy perfectly clear to me?
5. Have I expressed my hopes and goals for the relationship?

This is not a love affair. It is a relationship where honesty and self-knowledge help everyone. And you should review this relationship (in person, if possible) at least twice a year.

Give Your Advisor a Fighting Chance

I F SOMEONE IS MANAGING YOUR MONEY AND charging you for his or her services, either trust his or her judgment or fire the person. I had a client some years ago, the head of a Chicago advertising agency, smart with his accounts, but much too emotional to make any money with his own investments. After managing funds for him over a four-year period with a great deal of success, I began to take some long-term profits for him in some of the stocks I had chosen.

"What are you doing?" he yelled at me over the phone. "Selling that Houghton Mifflin, that Box Energy."

"Time to take a little money off the table," I said. "Remember, this is a discretionary account."

"But those were my babies. Next time consult with me when you're selling."

The advertising man had fallen in love with his stocks, and worse, after four years of ownership, he believed he had picked them.

If you choose someone to run your money, it is going to take about three years before you know if the manager is true to his or her basic stated philosophy, and if he or she is any good at what he or she does. I say three years because, generally, in that time frame, you see all sorts of markets—some good, some scary—and you can judge over that period how the manager reacts to all conditions.

You will muddy the waters if you second guess your advisor and, if after three years they are doing their job, don't interfere. If they're not, that period was a good test, and perhaps it's time to move on.

IT'S YOUR
MONEY

Risky Business

WHENEVER I MAKE A FINANCIAL DECISION FOR my family, myself, or my clients, I always ask, "What's the worst thing that can happen if this goes wrong?" And if I can live with my assessment of the downside, looked at from as many angles as possible, then the worst case will probably never happen, and I proceed with the investment or the financial move (like buying that house or investing in that private partnership).

I have, over my adult life, invested in movie production, a trotter horse, restaurants, rental units, commercial real estate, oil and gas, an improvisational theater group, a student and travel study program, and various other risk oriented moves.

When figuring my net worth (which we all do, all the time, for various reasons), I always valued my private investments at zero. Most of the time that valuation proved to be wise. Part of the reason I did this investing was emotional: I was involved with the people who were running the project.

One movie producer took me high into the Hollywood hills one magic night, hugged me around the shoulders, and pointed out the thousands of lights below us. "There's the magic," he told me, "the dream of the three cherries. I want that jackpot for you; I want it for me. Ca-ching." I was sucked into his dream. But for an amount that would not jeopardize my family or me. If it worked, wonderful. If it didn't, I could always use a tax loss. And the adventures were priceless. The producer disappeared at one point, off to a guru in Topanga Canyon who would teach him a better life, one that also did hold out the dream of the three cherries. But only in a spiritual sense. Ca-ching.

Most of this kind of investing is for the adventure, the experience, and the education—particularly, the education. No one can tell us anything in life and have it really sink in. We have to make our own mistakes. If we pay attention, we try never to make the same mistakes again. "Fool me once, shame on you," the saying goes, "fool me twice, shame on me."

I follow one primary rule of thumb when I make investments (or speculations) outside the stock market: I do it only when I have access to the people who are trying to make it work or who own the business. I will never do a deal with a promoter or marketing person.

Always do business with the principals in a deal. If you lose, so be it. But you will have access to the people who count, and it can truly be a learning experience. I believe in keeping a notebook if you ever make a private investment. In the notebook, you should keep track of what people promised or projected so that, as the deal progresses or flops, you have your reality check. It is also wonderfully constructive to look back on what could have been. And you will discover a lot about yourself in the process. Remember that probably no one will make you rich but you yourself. And also remember what Friedrich Nietzsche said, "That which doesn't kill me, will make me stronger."

Making Instant Enemies

D O YOU REMEMBER IN HIGH SCHOOL OR college ever fixing up a friend with a date? You thought you would be doing both of these people a favor. Then, it turned out, that somewhere down the line, both of the people ended up angry with you, and you'd lose two friends over what should have been a happy situation.

If you're not in the investment business, never give anyone financial advice, especially stock tips. You can't win on this deal. If the stock goes up, your friend is likely to say, "Gee, if you knew it was going to be that good, why didn't you tell me to buy more?" And if the stock goes down, you're a bum and the friend resents it. I get paid for giving advice and counsel. Don't take a chance on losing a friend because you're trying to do a good deed. And if the tips come from within your family, you run the risk of a double disaster—you'll be on the outs with both a friend and a family member.

Another good way to turn someone into an instant enemy is to loan him or her money. I have never had a good experience loaning money to others. The process is usually embarrassing to the friend or relative who asks. And he or she resents you whether or not you grant the loan. It usually means that you're going to lose that friend. One of my clients says, "The only upside to loaning money is if you want to get rid of a pain in the ass, loan them money. You'll probably never hear from them again." The same client has a method of dealing with anyone asking for money for any reason—whether a loan, an investment, or a donation.

"I'm terrible with money, a loose cannon," he would say. "So virtually everything in my life is in trust. You can call my trustee and ask him if it can be done. But my trustee is really a difficult person. I call him Dr. No. But if you care to, you can give him a try." My client is making this up. He has no trustee.

I have served this role of mythical trustee for my clients dozens of times. I am happy to be the bad guy, and no one ever bothers my clients twice. "You'll have to ask my trustee," is a great line for you to remember.

The Income-Plus Strategy

THE BIGGEST PROBLEM FACED BY NEWLY RETIRED people who have led active business lives is having to substitute investment income for the paychecks they received over their 25 to 40 years of working. They miss that regular paycheck. Their mindset is one of fear, regardless of the retirement funds that they have set aside.

Many retirees dwell too much on the income side of their retirement, with almost no thought to the growth side of the equation. Because of the decline in interest rates over the last ten years, people living on income from bonds have seen their annual incomes shrink. You could get 10 percent on long-term treasuries if you feared the stock market in 1987. Now long-term (30-year) rates are less than 6 percent. And they don't know what to do about it. My answer is the income-plus strategy.

Assume that you feel you have enough income flow to meet your annual budget. I will guarantee that every year will bring an unusual need, something you did not anticipate, that throws that budget off: a new roof, a new septic system, an emergency loan or gift to children or relatives, a special vacation.

If you anticipate spending, after tax, $100,000 per year, there will always be something that requires an additional $10,000 to $15,000 to $20,000 that you hadn't counted on spending. It's called "life."

Where do you get that overage? I will buy retired clients relatively large amounts of shares in companies I feel can grow their prices at 8 to 10 percent a year, while paying dividends of anywhere from 3 to 6 percent. This can usually give them a total return of from 11 to 16 percent annually. I have done this in the past with the Baby Bells, liquid master limited partnerships like Pimco, real estate investment trusts, selected utility stocks, and particularly in the last five years, GTE and the Baby Bells, and even, when the drug stocks were out of favor, with Bristol Myers.

The retired people got their dividends and have seen their monies growing nicely. The extras that they need I provide by selling off odd amounts of appreciated shares, little by little: 20 shares here, 50 shares there, to get them the annual kicker that they need.

I pick companies in this program where I feel I can't be penalized too much in bad markets, and where the dividend yields will protect the downside. Obviously, in greedy markets, it is tougher and tougher to find the right yield-plus securities. But with patience and someone who is smart helping you, you can go a long way toward enhancing your retirement planning, getting the funds you need for the quality of life you want, and growing the pot for your beneficiaries in the future.

You have to be more creative with your money today than ever before, with so many choices, and so much misinformation. Do not be fixated on needing, for instance, $40,000 a year income, when your portfolio yields only $25,000. If you manage the portfolio correctly, the extras you need can come from growth.

You've Got Better Things to Do Than Retire

CAN YOU PLAY GOLF FIVE OR SIX DAYS A WEEK? I don't think so.

I had a client years ago who was CEO of a manufacturing company that was bought out by a conglomerate. He was paid $17 million for his business, and, with glee, he retired to Palm Beach. While he ran his company he employed almost 300 people, and he was a powerful man in his community, serving on many boards. Three months after he retired, he called me. "I'm depressed," he said.

"How can you be depressed?" I asked him. "You told me you had it made."

I heard a large sigh on the other end of the line. "I'm worth $17 million," he said. "And people don't return my phone calls. What am I going to do? Doomed to walk three paces behind my wife into eternity?" He died within the next six months.

It is not the amount of money someone has; it is about how his or her power is perceived. Without one's center of power, the money means nothing; it isn't taken seriously. Here's one sad fact of our society at the end of the 20th century: Not enough honor is given to age and experience. A friend in the auto business told me recently that Lee Iacocca, the former chairman of Chrysler, has found that the biggest problem he was having with retirement was the horrible feeling of having to fly on commercial airlines like everyone else. We're not going to hold any benefits for Lee Iacocca, but feeling that one is out of the loop is a dangerous and sad situation for retired people.

Many times, especially these days, people have no choice in when they retire. They don't look forward to it, but they have been "downsized," out of work at a relatively early age. One of my college classmates had this experience and told me, "I spent a year interviewing, went through friends back to grammar school, used my entire Rolodex and then some. Many days I'd sit in the lobby of the Plaza Hotel between appointments, using the men's room there, and the phones, staring at the people checking in and out. I've never been so depressed in my life. After all those years with the company, the lobby of the Plaza was my only office."

We live in an America where, for better or worse, we are defined by what we do. "What do you do?" women began being asked first in the 1970s, and many of them were embarrassed, because of the pressure of the times, to say, "I'm at home with the children." Today, the same kind of embarrassment is felt as everyone, it seems, is asking, "What is your e-mail address?" God forbid you don't have one.

One of my beliefs is that the adrenaline pumps if you have purpose in life, and that purpose helps in giving us good health and long life. Look how many artists, writers, musicians, seem, on average, to live to great age. My cardiologist tells me that his office advises all of their patients, "Never retire."

I recommend that retired businesspeople who feel unfulfilled pursue the nonprofit arena, charities and schools, particularly in fundraising efforts. Through membership in various nonprofit organizations, I have known dozens of "development" people, most of whom are almost totally unprepared for raising money. With their experience in business, and their usually quite large circle of acquaintances, retired people would be a major plus for nonprofit fundraising. But they must be paid for their efforts. You have to feel you are valued in life by more than a pat on the back and a "Thanks."

I have another idea for people who are from 55 to 65 years old and have had successful business careers. Apply for training programs at the large investment firms that farm clients' funds, the so-called wrap accounts, out to professional money managers for a fee.

If you have retired early and you're not happy about it, and you believe you can be productive for another 10 or 15 years, think about this: You have friends, business colleagues, a vast circle of acquaintances going back over 30 or 40 years of business life. Many of those people, believe me, have gotten mediocre or even bad financial advice. Trust your instincts; learn which money managers or funds can benefit from your incredible Rolodex—and match your contacts to places that can improve their financial lives, while you act as quarterback.

If the investment firm is smart, they'll hire you in a minute. And you know about giving service and personal attention. That's what most people want more than anything else. And if I ran a major brokerage firm, I'd much rather get ten good productive years out of a professional than see 80 percent of our young-blood trainees quit the business or run off to my competitors within two years.

Retirement Income Tricks

"MOST RETIRED PEOPLE HOLD STOCKS AS WELL as bonds," one of the smartest institutional bond managers in America has told me. "So there are many strategies you can use. Don't fool around if you want the highest yield with bonds," he said. "Go out as long as you want, 30 years or more, buy and lock in the largest returns."

(The longer the maturity of a bond, usually, the higher the coupon, or interest rate. For instance, currently, if you buy a long-term telephone bond, like the AT&T 8 1/8 percents, maturing in 2022, your current return will be approximately 7.69 percent. Contrast this yield to a five-year bond of comparable quality and you drop to a 5.8 percent current return.)

"Obviously you get the biggest swings in price with the longest bond maturities," said my legendary bond manager. "These are the riskiest bonds if you are going to trade them and not hold them to maturity. I say buy the highest yield bonds, and if rates rise and your bonds drop in price, assess your total tax situation at the end of each year. Chances are, you've taken some profits in your stocks. If so, sell your long-term bonds. Balance your profits by taking losses in your bonds. Then rebuy long-term bonds at the new, higher rates."

Most people never think of using bonds when they need losses. If you haven't taken any stock profits in the year, you may want to pin some gains down in long-held, low-cost equities and use the bond losses against them. Using these strategies, you'll both add to your income and have been smart about tax planning at the same time.

Your Children's Money

THERE ARE A MILLION WAYS TO THE TRUTH IN money management, and no such thing as the pure way. And if you're raising children and facing serious tuition prospects, here are a few guidelines I follow in advising parents.

Of course, college education today can cost as much as $30,000 annually. And that's before you buy a book, much less the computer-related outlays that are standard in academia today. If you take the route into private education earlier, at the high school level, the costs are still mind-boggling. Boarding schools, like Middlesex, in Concord, Massachusetts, can charge more than $24,000 a year. And because many parents insist that Junior and

Missy start the fast track even earlier, preschool and private grammar schools can set you back $10,000 a year.

I believe in a three-pronged approach to investing for a child's education. My approach is efficient and practical. Start with U.S. Treasury zero coupon bonds. These bonds pay no interest in cash. You buy them at a discount, say, 30 cents on the dollar. They mature at face value in a specified time frame. This way you can target maturities to match your requirements: so much coming due to coincide with freshman year in college, sophomore year, and so on. The rates are guaranteed by the government at time of purchase.

Currently, money doubles in these instruments in 11 years so that $5,000 automatically becomes $10,000 in May, 2010. This works out to be about 5.9 percent annually. Not so hot, you say? Perhaps, but it makes sure that part of the tuition is taken care of automatically, and you don't have to suffer through the sometimes (believe it or not) negative bias of stock markets. Peace of mind means more than anything else in financial planning; there should be a conservative part to this process. And that means zero coupon bonds.

The second part of investing for children's education involves periodic purchases of a good growth mutual fund. Monies should probably be systematically added to the fund so that you can take advantage of dollar cost averaging (putting similar amounts in annually, often when prices are lower and more shares can be bought). Any financial consultant can give you long-term records of all the mutual funds. The earlier in a child's life you start this program, the better it will work. Over time, this part of the plan is designed to grow in value faster than the zero coupons, but with more risk.

The third section is the most aggressive part, and like the growth mutual fund, it requires patience and discipline. It involves owning shares in a stake in life company. This involves foresight and originality as well because to justify buying shares in one company over time, even in small amounts, you must feel (or your advisor feels) that it can have dynamic growth over a 20-year period.

Imagine if you had done this over the last 20 years with Coca Cola, General Electric, or Gillette. Perhaps your company will be Microsoft or Intel, if you believe in them enough. I'd bet on Lucent Technologies, myself. The former telecommunications equipment side of the old AT&T, Lucent also owns Bell Laboratories, arguably the greatest research facility in the world. Keep buying your stake in life company and pray for bad markets periodically, when you can buy shares cheaper. Obviously an Internet company would fill the bill here. But you better make sure you're confident of the survival of the one you pick.

Put your plan into action—the earlier, the better. Invest at the same time each year, like a child's birthday, or during the holidays. It makes it simpler to remember and becomes automatic. Paying for your child's education will become remarkably painless, and if you pick the right stake in life company, your child could end up richer than you. Isn't that what every parent dreams? My daughter the doctor.

The simplest form of an account for children is the custodian account. It is as easy to open as knowing the child's name and having a proper Social Security number: James Smith, custodian for Sarah Smith under the Massachusetts Uniform Gifts to Minors Act. Every state has its own uniform gifts act, and it is one of the few legal adventures you can perform yourself, without the use of a lawyer. In this case, James Smith acts as custodian of his daughter Sarah's assets until she reaches her majority. (In Massachusetts, it's 18, and I'm not here to argue the merits or mistakes of this policy. But think back to when you were 18 and what you would have done if a wad of dough were dropped in your lap.)

The best advice I can give parents is to start a custodian account at the earliest possible moment in the child's life. If things are tight for you, push the grandparent button. Do not, as the child grows older, ever tell your child what funds are accruing for him or her. Memo to Cambridge, Massachusetts, or East Side of New York residents: Try to resist treating your children as "little adults" and revealing all to them at an early age. Trust me, they cannot handle it. And they are best served thinking they have to go out and create their own wealth.

I remember when I actually got my first car my sophomore year in college. I was washing my Volkswagen bug (gray with a hand-painted red stripe) in the driveway that spring break, and my father came out to watch. I don't know what possessed me, but I looked at him and said, "Out of your clutches, my lord."

My father went into orbit. I apologized. But wheels definitely meant freedom. And if I had come into possession of a custodial account at that time, I guarantee it would not have been a Volkswagen bug. It would have been a Corvette, or more likely, a classic MG.

I have friends who have kept their children's custodial accounts going until the kids are into their 30s. My friend Max is one of those.

"I told them years ago that they had a college fund," Max said. "I know that the true age that my children can be told that they have 'certain expectations' is 30 years old."

"Why 30?" I asked.

"Because," Max explained, "by 30, we all have taken some hits in life. We've had failures and disappointments, and perhaps we've learned from them. Also, it's the age when maybe they're getting married, or buying a condo, or starting a business. They're not so likely to blow it on a Porsche. But at 30, if they do blow it, they possibly deserve it. Before then, they just don't have enough history."

The 1997 tax reform legislation has provided for a so-called Education IRA. Parents can contribute up to $500 annually to a plan for each child under 18 that can grow tax free and be distributed tax free for the purpose of higher education. There are restrictions on the Education IRA that you should check with a financial advisor. The restrictions do not allow contributions from individuals with adjusted gross income of more than $95,000, or from couples who make more than $150,000. For you people, max out on the custodial accounts, and as Blanche DuBois did, trust in the kindness of strangers—that is, the friends, relatives, and other people who interact with your kids.

Estate Planning

I HAVE A WONDERFUL FRIEND NAMED WILLY, THE kind of man people turn to if they need support. He was a catcher on the baseball team in college, a tough leader who could be counted on to lead the cheers or block the plate as the situation demanded. And he had lots of friends scattered around the globe as he prospered in life as an executive with a paper products company. As Willy got into his 50s, he told me at lunch one day that many of these friends started to do estate planning for the first time, and thought it would be a wonderful idea to have someone as solid as Willy as the executor of their wills and a trustee of the trusts drawn up for their beneficiaries. "You know," Willy told me at lunch, "I told several older friends of my parents that I would serve in these capacities for them. They were great people, and I believe in being a good friend. But it turns out that you know the donor, the parent. But you don't have any idea who the Goddamn beneficiaries really are, on a personal basis. Or how greedy or unbelievable they can be."

"Money always draws a crowd," I agreed with him.

"Listen to this story," Willy said, "and think twice before you ever accept the role of trustee or executor. One of my father's college classmates was dying of cancer, and he asked to see me. 'My two boys have disappointed me,' he said. 'They've gone on strange routes in life, and they'll need guidance and a gentle spirit. Would you oversee their affairs and make sure they get solid advice? I remember how you used to throw out runners, trying to steal second base; you'll be just the ticket for my boys.'

"One of the boys would get his money outright. He was married, living in Italy with an Italian bride, running an export–import business. No problem, I thought, even though his dad had told me that the boy was 'somewhat unstable.' The other son had taken a Buddhist name, Krishna Bul, and was currently trekking in Nepal. He evidently was working out some laying on of the hands therapy for the ills of the world. His money was to be kept in trust with the income doled out carefully. He could get principal payments for special needs.

"Pretty simple, I thought at the time. When the father died," Willy went on, "the faxes started to come from Italy.

And the long, convoluted letters from Nepal, then India, then Taos, New Mexico, with nonnegotiable demands in very non-Buddhist language from Krishna Bul.

"First, old Krishna wanted a gold American Express card in his Buddhist nickname only. Which was Lum. Then he wanted a distribution of $25,000 to make a video of him doing special massage therapy using only the thumbs. . . . 'Lum's Thumbs,' he called it."

"Next thing you know," Willy went on, "both of the ingrates are suing me for not performing my fiduciary duty, which as they saw it, meant handing them the money. . . . No good deed goes unpunished."

I have to go to Palm Beach to meet with my estate lawyer. He doesn't live there, but he does love to wander in places where the rich and famous go to play my lawyer" I mention.

"Great estate lawyers are voyeurs," he tells me. "They never participate in life; they observe it."

My estate lawyer's name is Peter, and he answers all four of my requirements for people who are on my personal team:

1. He was originally recommended to me by very smart friends.
2. Peter is quirky; a character, whose main talent in life is his understanding of human nature.
3. The syndicated columnist Ellen Goodman told me years ago that she wanted people working for

her who are obsessive-compulsive, who are workaholics. "They need to take care of me before they take care of themselves. They can't help it. Horrible way to live, but great for the people they care for."

Peter is obsessive-compulsive. He dates when he is in Palm Beach, and he always dines in the same restaurant so the service will be assured. He keeps several Ferragamo scarves with the bartender, whom he has taken care of in advance. Peter sits at the bar with each new date, and if the first round of drinks goes well, he will say, "This is a magic bar for the right people." He signals the bartender. "See what happens here, if you have the look." Then the bartender produces the beautifully wrapped package containing the Ferragamo scarf.

"Don't dump on the poor wills and estate lawyer," Peter has said to me. "Yes, it's corny. But the attention to detail is like being a goddamn set designer. That's why people come from all over the world to have me do their estates."

4. He is younger than I am. You have to start developing your experts who are going to pay attention to you, who are at least a few years your junior. You want people on your team who are very much in the hunt professionally.

Over the last several years, Peter has made his estate plan principles very clear. I'm sure the practical you will find these principles valuable:

1. If you are truly rich, estate planning is done by the accumulation of control and power, not through the accumulation of assets.

2. Choose that person for your trustee or executor whom you trust most in the world. It is an act of conferring power, and it becomes the ultimate act of love for a man to give his wife that power.

3. A client should never make his lawyer the trustee; there are too many conflicts of interest. And never duplicate the roles of the people who serve you. Your trustee, lawyer, and money manager should all be separate people.

4. Always pay your lawyer by the hour, never by the size of the estate.

5. The biggest mistake you can make is making a corporate lawyer your trustee. Think about the word *trustee*; he or she is someone you should trust completely because often a trustee's primary responsibility is to hire and fire other professionals who are working in your behalf.

6. Never make a bank or an institution your trustee. They charge big fees, and they cannot organize toilet paper. Furthermore, never make any professional your executor. Make it a *personal* relationship.

7. If you want to live like the rich people live, start signing your name as trustee, as opposed to owner, early in life. People of substantial wealth have their own names on nothing.

8. My number one goal is, "Do no harm." Lawyers have a penchant for doing more harm than good; I'm sorry, but it's true. Don't make it worse. Most lawyers think they know the answers; the client knows the answers—your lawyer needs to know the questions.

9. When you hire a lawyer to do a will or trusts for you, make sure he or she is practical. So often estate lawyers give you their last client's plan: It's a nice pair of shoes, but it doesn't fit you. Get referrals when you search for a lawyer, and if common sense seems to be lacking, go elsewhere.

Peter is a sensitive man who would throttle me if I even suggested that the following were true. "I'm a loner," he has told me. "Christmas is not my holiday, so I work on Christmas day. I also work on New Year's Day."

"I've created a list," he told me. "Originally, it was for my sons when they got out of high school and can start to pay attention to the realities of life." He calls his list, "Stop Living Like a Stupid Person: Two Hundred and Fifty Common Mistakes Even You Can Avoid." As an example of his quirky but wonderful thought processes, here are several of the items on his list of stupid things to avoid:

1. Don't try to outsmart the professionals.
2. Don't pay extra to extend the factory warranty.
3. Don't ignore the directions and follow your hunch.
4. Don't go up on your roof to check out the problem first.
5. Don't read *Walden*.
6. Don't ask your father about his sex life.
7. Don't move to Buffalo for a better job.

You get the picture.

Peter showed up one day in my office in what looked like the military uniform of what used to be called a Banana Republic. The blue woolen jacket had braid on the shoulders and epaulets. Ribbons and medals adorned his left breast.

"What's this?" I asked Peter.

"Once a year," he told me, "I put on the uniform of Montenegro, tiny little Montenegro on the Adriatic Sea. And I wear what I think the Great Gatsby wore when he was decorated by Montenegro in the First World War. Then I wander around thinking about romance and lost love, and Gatsby."

"I can't think of a better way to spend a day," I told him. Of course, I knew he was just taking a break—in his obsessive-compulsive way—from helping his clients. So he paraded around the office for a while, showing off his uniform jacket. Then he sighed and headed for the door, paused, and said to me, "One more thing. Never use a lawyer whose character is not as good as yours."

LESSONS
FROM
HISTORY

Losing My Virginity

ONE CRISIS I WAS WITNESS TO—WHICH reinforces the importance of knowing history—was the assassination of John F. Kennedy in November 1963. By then, I was a practicing stockbroker, living at my parents' house. But the resident manager kept me on a modest salary ($85 a week) even though I also filled in for the teletype operator and did odd jobs like changing the cellophane tape on the Translux ticker machines that ran all day, printing the trades on the New York Stock Exchange. In those days, rolls of tape were changed manually, and ink cartridges were inserted into slots so the printing action became legible. Changing the rolls and the ink cartridges was my job. And I have always been a mechanically challenged person. Virtually every day, I would go home with my arms blue with ink up to my elbows. "I've heard of blue-collar workers, but this is ridiculous," my mother would say.

"The resident manager says it builds character to know all the jobs in the office." I would tell her. "And the $85 a week is gravy."

"The gravy is on your tie," she would say. Mother always got the last word.

I was changing the ink rolls when the rumor first broke about JFK. The brokers began screaming at me, "Get those inkers in; we can't see." The ticker tape was running with indistinct images. They needed the ink man to make the numbers real. And the numbers were falling as the rumors of the shooting became fact. Most people, I believe, when facing chaos, think of self-preservation. Heroes are the ones who look to save others. The brokers were still yelling; people from other offices on our floor streamed into our boardroom to watch the falling market—everyone shocked by the news, gathering together to be somehow reassured by human contact. I was a rookie at this point in my career, and with panic building around me, my initial reaction was, "It's over, my brief career, the stock market, the country in turmoil." The resident manager beckoned me with a finger into his office.

"You think it's over, don't you?" he said.

"I really don't know what to think."

"Did you ever take an American History course?"

I admitted that I had.

"Then you have to step back and recognize that we have this wonderful thing called a Constitution. This incredible event will pass as far as markets are concerned.

We have succession in place, and form, and people of enormous goodwill. Always bet against the crowd. There is a poet named David McCord who wrote about Harvard: 'Is that you, John Harvard? I said to his statue.

Aye, that's me, said John, and after you're gone.' It's true about Harvard," the manager said. "And it's true about America. Be a buyer."

That lesson has been fundamental in my investment decisions and should be equally fundamental in yours. Go against the popular mood when there is desperation around you.

I had another lesson that day, almost the flip side of being a buyer in chaotic times. A young client of mine came into the office, someone my mother would have called "swervy." He had been a lacrosse player in college with a reputation for dirty play.

"Kennedy's been shot," he said.

"It's unbelievable." I answered.

"What can we sell short?" he asked. "Chance here to make a score."

I remember the Rothschilds getting carrier pigeon reports of Wellington's victory at Waterloo and going long the British pound before the world knew the results of that battle. Would the SEC have called that inside information?

But I stared at my client, not really believing he had suggested selling short (betting against the market) at such an emotional time.

"I don't want your business." I said.

"You're a sucker," he said. "Suckers don't win ball-games." And he walked out. I was a young broker, naïve perhaps, but it was my first brush with immorality in business. I told the resident partner about it, and he smiled. "You lose your virginity, I think, three times in life," he said. "The first is when you lose it in a physical sense. The second, like today, in a business sense, and you realize that the world is not necessarily an honorable place." He hesitated.

"And the third?" I asked.

"Don't call me a cynic. But the third time you lose your virginity is the day you get married. You'll see what I mean." And he went back to his battle station on the phones.

The Long View

WHEN I WAS A YOUNG TRAINEE ON WALL Street, I lived in a resident hotel room where, if I lay down on the floor and stretched out, I could touch my toes to one wall and my fingers to the other. I shared a bathroom with someone I never met, and there was a sink in one corner of the room, a view out of the window of an airshaft, and the sound at night, as I wondered if I would ever really make a living, of roaches scurrying around my sorry room. I'd take the Lexington Avenue subway down to Wall Street, and when I started training, I was given a key role at my firm, collating and stapling together research reports. One of the analysts, Sam Londoner, an old-timer who was the in-house expert on railroads, used to drop in, watch me for a while, and smile.

"I used to lick envelopes when I was training," he said. "Actually lick them because our boss wanted us to pay our dues. You probably get to use a sponge." Londoner wore no wristwatch. He used a train conductor's old, large pocket watch, which he kept on a thick silver chain with every link hallmarked. "It belonged to a conductor who was supposedly killed in a train robbery out West by the James boys, Jesse and Frank."

He had been on Wall Street since the 1930s, the Depression years. During my months in New York, he often took me out to lunch, introducing me to Manhattan clam chowder, made with a tomato base, instead of cream. "If you want a rich, long life," he would tell me, "you have to learn to pace yourself. That way, you can do what you love to do almost forever. Just remember this story," he said. And I have. "Two bulls stood at the top of a hill," Londoner told me. "One old bull and a young one. At the bottom of the hill were about a dozen cows. The young bull was pawing the ground. 'Let's run down the hill and mount one,' the young bull cried. The old bull shook his head. 'Let's walk down the hill,' he advised, 'and mount them all.'"

I admit that I love to listen to stories of the past. I know that, in part, I'm looking for ways to avoid making the same mistakes in my own life.

I think in this new century, in an increasingly anonymous world, we need more than ever before people to counsel us, people to care. For years, I have asked myself who, of the hundreds of people I have known who watch over others' money, I would use for advice if I were not in the business myself. The few people I have identified all have years of experience; they all read books; they all know history. These are some of my prejudices in seeking investment advisors. One of my favorites in these regards is Johnny Minot.

A wonderful thing about the retail stock brokerage business is that you never need to retire. "I'd like to go like Arthur Thornhill" (one-time chairman of Little, Brown publishers), Johnny Minot once said to me. "He died nursing his second martini at lunch in Locke Ober's, the old restaurant in Boston. For a week after that, they kept his table unoccupied, just a place setting and a martini, in his memory."

Everything reminds Johnny Minot of a story. He was once the senior partner of one of Boston's oldest investment firms, one of the many that went south in the paperwork crises of the early 1970s. I met him shortly thereafter, ensconced in a new firm. (People who are always reminded of stories usually land on their feet.)

"You look like a million bucks," I said to him, admiring his style.

"Is that all?" he answered, laughing with me. Johnny Minot is an old-timer in the securities business. But at 77 years, he seems, like most people who love what they do, much younger than he is. Every day he wears in his lapel a flower that he buys fresh on his morning walks through the market district. "I like to watch businesses starting up in the day," he says, "washing down sidewalks, opening shutters, putting out merchandise for display. Most people in the securities business think that the stock market is numbers on a screen. Well, it's people opening shutters, really. Companies make things, employ people. If you advise people about their money, you've got to appreciate how companies operate, and understand that people make the companies work. And you've got to walk in the market-place to appreciate how money works."

Johnny Minot came into the investment business in the late 1940s, and he was paid $50 a week. "This was called OJT, on-the-job-training," he explained. "I helped on the teletype machine entering orders and sending messages to New York. I chalked up the board where quotations were monitored then and could be seen by the entire office. There were no Quotrons, no immediate communication; everything was figured by hand. I even used the hand signals used on the curb, the American

Stock Exchange, taught me by a girlfriend whose father was a floor member. She told me that with the hand signals we could always communicate in a crowded party without anyone else knowing what we were saying. She also said that the true test of a relationship was if it survived a train ride from New York to Boston. If you were not bored during that trip—you had something."

I asked Minot about cold calling—calling people away from dinner, doctors out of operations, priests out of services to offer "investment opportunities"—a practice that seems so nastily prevalent in the securities industry today.

"I believe in face-to-face dealings," Johnny said. "I've never made a so-called cold call in my 40 years in business. What I did when I was a young broker is this. . . ." He took off one of his shoes and held up the sole to me.

"I walked over to the leather district, around Lincoln Street, and went into the office buildings. I started on the top floor of each, visited every office, and asked to speak with the boss. I did the same with all the wool brokers. Boston was the center of the wool trade in those days, and the dress manufacturers were in Chinatown on Kneeland Street.

"Almost everyone talked with me because I was an enterprising young man and because people find it difficult to refuse human contact. That's how I built my business. I used to write down what they were interested in so I could personalize things when I came back to them.

"My father had told me, 'A short pencil is better than a long memory.' People love it if you remember that they like baseball or that their wives come from Memphis or what their kids' names are. Write it down. It's obvious that the cold callers of today," Johnny went on, "are interested in the commission, the short-term play, and not the long-term relationships. Most of them will have short-term relationships with the securities industry."

"Do you blame the 1980s for this attitude?" I asked him.

"The '80s were just a greed blip," Johnny answered. "There's something more serious going on demographically. It has to do with standards, and—I hate to bring this up but—family values has a lot to do with it also.

"Someone told me recently," he said, "about a brokerage office in Boston where they have repeatedly posted signs in the men's room concerning the filthy mess there. Toilets were not flushed; newspapers and towels were consistently left scattered on the floors. They were fouling their own nest. When I heard about this, I figured that no one had ever taught them right from wrong, no one had ever set standards for them or let them know what was expected."

I asked Johnny what the biggest changes have been in the investment business in the last 40 years.

"The biggest single change," he said, "is in the role of the stockbroker. Stockbrokers used to be family counselors, as useful to people as a doctor or a lawyer. It was a respected profession. In Boston, of course, the business was the place to dump the dumb brother or cousin. Many WASPs from old families were buried in investment firms, places they'd go until it was time to go to the club for lunch and disappear for the afternoon. Even in the late '50s, there was almost no ethnic diversity in the investment business in Boston; a handful of Jewish brokers, the Irish mostly in the back office or on trading desks. At Hornblower and Weeks, early in the '60s, they hired a handful of Jewish and Armenian guys as brokers, put them in a line in the boardroom. They called it the 'Gaza Strip.' Today, of course, it's like America. Everybody into the pool. The way it should be."

"At least you see some pluses about the modern investment climate."

"Well," he said, "where we used to be counselors and advisors, the new brokers are 'asset gatherers,' urged to bring in as much money into the firm as they can so the investment firms can get cradle-to-grave control."

"Is that bad?" I asked.

"Not if they were being taught to serve the whole client. Until recently, many of the major firms' training programs taught only one thing: phone sales techniques. As the young people say, 'Gimme a break.' Those kids couldn't analyze a company, rip apart a balance sheet, if their lives depended on it. They read from prepared scripts, for God's sake."

"So what's the future of the investment business? What forms will it take?"

"Well, I know I'm a dinosaur, so it's dangerous to preach about the past. You don't want anyone to say, 'It's old Minot and his sour grapes.' I also know that in business you have to change or die. Jordan Marsh wouldn't change as a retailer. They're dead. IBM's another example. They had to change, or die.

"I see things breaking down into three areas. One, the mutual funds—fine for anyone who doesn't need human contact. Two, the old-fashioned counseling business coming back into favor—stockbrokers dispensing long-term advice for a fee, with commissions diminishing in importance. And three, people taking a part of their money, perhaps 10 percent, to try to do it themselves online. I say 10 percent because, in my opinion, after they do it for awhile, they'll learn how difficult it is and go back to their real jobs. But a piece of most people's money will remain for individual messing around.

"The big secret to the capitalist system is to give more people a piece of the pie. This is happening via the pension plans. With literally millions of workers in all sorts of company plans buying stocks and bonds, you will eventually see the Dow Jones at 20,000. Young brokers should start becoming experts in estate planning and taxes. There is huge growth coming if you know these areas."

"Are you an optimist on the future of America, aside from stock markets?"

Minot adjusted his boutonniere and smiled again. "In this country, it used to be like there was a wagon with one person in it with a hurt leg and nine people pulling the wagon. Easy. Now it seems like there are seven people in the wagon and only two pulling. Hard."

"Last thoughts about the investment business?"

"Sure. If you work hard, you will pass 95 percent of your competition. And, given time, investment company research departments could break the Bank of England."

"And if you had to define the business you've been in for 40 years?"

Johnny Minot thought briefly and looked at his watch. You could only philosophize for so long. "It's a hard way to make an easy living," he said, and got up to go see a client in person.

The Crash of '87

THE *BOSTON GLOBE* PUBLISHED MY ACCOUNT of the Crash of '87 on its op-ed page: Here is a piece of it:

"I felt sick to my stomach when I walked into my building on Monday morning, October 19. My office has the best view of Boston, 39 floors up, across the harbor and out to the Charles River. Secretaries were joking about the weekend; young brokers were shooting the breeze. They didn't realize what was at stake; they didn't understand. I felt like someone who had just been told he had something incurable and no one else could appreciate it. I lost all my money in 1972 when my old company bellied up in the collapse of so many Wall Street firms and the Dow Jones averages read like the combined weight of two NFL linebackers. I couldn't stand going through it again, and I swear I saw images of blood in the river below me."

Perhaps extreme, but I was in the eye of the storm.

After the previous Friday's historic drop of 108 points, I knew my ordinarily complacent clients would be lined up to hear my reactions. I was in at 8:00 AM, and there were already 27 yellow call-back slips on my desk. I have more than 1,700 clients, from Hong Kong to London to Aspen, people of intelligence and goodwill, not too greedy in good times, relatively cool in adversity. Their combined portfolios at the end of August 1987 stood at almost $130 million. My clients are an eclectic mix of professionals, from board chairmen to Pulitzer Prize winners to ex-KGB agents to cab drivers. They give me feedback about what Americans are thinking more than practically any manager of money in the country, certainly more than any psychiatrist. What if they all called today? No more could I run an orderly business. It would be out of control. And it was.

As the selling frenzy started, my friend Bert called from Marin County. Bert has money scattered among five money managers around the globe and switches them every two years. "They're a bunch of fools," he would say periodically. "I would get the big hype, and none of them are worth spit in performance. I should manage the dough myself. But I found this new guy in Nebraska. It's the heartland for me from now on." Bert has these managers place their orders through me because he likes me and understands that we can't be switching friends every two years. "I won't even ask about the market," he says. "But I like the Cardinals in the series." The jokes stopped early in the day.

Shoe manufacturers are traditionally the biggest shooters in the market. My client Solly called when the Dow was down 150 points. Solly has been my bellwether for years, calling every major turn absolutely wrong. He buys at the top, sells at the bottom. What he loses in the market, he makes up by inventing new lasts, new lifts. "Don't buy anything, Solly," I pleaded. He wanted to buy Ford and General Motors. "You won't take an order, what kind of communist are you?" he asked. "I'm afraid if you buy today," I said, "we'll all burn in hell." It was a day for superstitions and praying to any God who would listen. I bought him the stock.

I saw this coming, I said to myself, as prices kept falling. I took a job from *Playboy* in July to write an article for their January issue on the subject, "What's the top of the market, when do you sell, and what do you do with the money?" I had already seen the signs—greed and indifference to restraint of any kind in government or in personal finance.

I also had the classic sign of a top: a space in my condominium garage last month sold for $100,000. Is there something wrong with a society where a place to put your car sells for $100,000? I knew what to sell short, how much to put into T-bills. I wrote this in August. But I thought I'd have time to make an orderly retreat. I thought that prices would go to extremes and run longer than the average smart person might think.

What did I do about it? I was about 10 percent in cash. Only Stanley the producer, my passionate Hollywood client, sold everything in the middle of the summer, with me yelling at him that he was too early. I passed this off to the fact that Stanley was about to become a father for the first time at age 50, that it was an emotional reaction. Stanley played a laugh track on the phone to me, and I felt like St. Augustine when the saint said, "Make me chaste, Lord. But not quite yet." I couldn't believe that years of progress were wiped out in a day.

Monday was the longest day of my life. Shock and shutdown set in around noon. My responses became automatic, and I hoped they sounded convincing. I had three assistants, and each of them was on the phones nonstop for the day spouting my party line: If you can afford to, wait; if you're not being squeezed on margin, then do not sell. During the Depression, the only people who got destroyed were those who could not service their debts. Get your debt down and stay calm. If you have free cash, buy a small amount of the best companies: Exxon, Mobil, General Electric, Gillette, AT&T., the GAP. Spend 20 to 25 percent of available funds and keep the rest in reserve.

Irving from Bel Air called. He was a robust 74-year-old. "Can I buy a new car?" he inquired.

"What kind?" I asked.

"A Cadillac."

"You're 74, Irving," I answered. "You've seen a lot more than I have. You can buy anything you want."

"Maybe I better lease," he said.

The evening of the crash I flew to New York for a dinner meeting I couldn't cancel. The entire day was like walking through a dream. I had no center; I was watching a Fellini movie, but I was in it at the same time. What I was doing was mourning. Not really for lost money, nor for lost innocence about the fact that the world can go mad. In a sense, I was mourning my stupidity: that I saw it all but could do nothing about it. There was no orderly retreat in a panic where our institutions could be crumbling.

I was also mourning for an America I thought that would be much changed when events calmed down. An entire generation of young people would hear a word with which they were totally unfamiliar: "No!"

I thought that every life would be affected, every business, from real estate to retail to auto sales and that Monday would prove to be a watershed in our history. We were going to have to do with less.

The plane trip was unusual. It was on time, and no one was really speaking to each other. My hotel was filled with Japanese. They were all bowing and smiling at one another as if this were truly the end of the Fellini movie.

My dinner tasted bitter and my stomach felt the bile. Occasionally, I took deep breaths to calm the adrenaline. I told a friend a week ago, "Things don't collapse when everyone is predicting it, when everyone is fearful. They collapse when you're feeling confident, when you're feeling smart."

"People are fearful," he said, "when they see a tidal wave coming. But it doesn't mean they can do anything about it." He was right.

A man wrote to the paper in rebuttal to my op-ed piece. "My heart bleeds for the poor stockbrokers, feeding off the people. They should all be in Hell, broke!" Perhaps there was some truth in that, I thought at the time. But no one had handed me my money. I had worked long and hard to make what I had. But, of course, I could protest in a revolution, all the way to the guillotine.

Two days after the crash, after my op-ed piece appeared in the paper, I was leaving for work in the morning and a jogger ran by me. The runner was a CEO of a public company, a large manufacturer of upholstered fabrics, and a smart man. He puffed by me and said, "I read your article. You worry too much. America is going to be just fine."

He was right about America, but he didn't have the small picture pinned down. Within a year, his wife sued him for divorce, claiming among other things, that he had attempted to poison her. His stock plummeted, and he saw half his net worth transferred to his ex. But America rolls on. Several years later, I ran into the CEO.

"Well," he said, "I know that George Bernard Shaw said, "The man who marries a second time didn't deserve to lose the first one.""

"Wasn't that Confucius?" I asked.

"Whoever. Anyway, I've married again. The stock is up, and we've got a little girl."

"At your age?" I questioned.

"Hey, it's given me renewal. Though," he admitted, "it's a little weird. I took my daughter for the old 'let's get into private school' routine. This exercise starts at pre-school, for God's sake. So I took her to this fancy place, saw the headmistress, and I said to her, 'Look, my kid can take anything. But I'm too old for rejection.'"

"You still feel good about America?"

"America is fine; it's the people who are screwed up."

History teaches us that you can never say "never" about anything. The Roman, Ottoman, and British empires can fall; the Berlin Wall can come down; fascism can rise; and we can have depressions in America. When dramatic events occur, you have to have a plan for yourself in the financial arena. In preparing for this, have a financial advisor who either majored in college in history, English, or philosophy, or took heavy course loads in these areas. Why? Because they have a sense of the past, of what was written and thought about, and that should give them some insight into human behavior. Because it is emotion more than anything else that moves markets: fear and greed. And I cannot repeat that often enough.

Always interview anyone who presumes to manage your money in person, and ask about his or her education and hobbies. You may often have need to call upon this financial person for help in other areas: referrals for doctors or lawyers, schools for children, letters for cooperative apartment purchases. Financial people have wide circles of acquaintances. Use these people, if they answer your requirements, for the value added that the best of them can provide. Calls to mutual funds will never get you a letter to a bank supporting your need for a mortgage—or get you through a crash.

PEOPLE

AND

MONEY

The Education of a
Stockbroker

KATIE WAS A PHILOSOPHER. WHEN FACED WITH
a problem, she would always say, "God is
good and Jack is fishin'. . . ."

Katie had the knack for love and the gift of laughter.
She arrived in Boston from Connemara, County Galway,
right after World War I, her only possession a gold sover-
eign dated 1907 with a glorified likeness of Edward VII on
one side, St. George and the dragon on the other. Like
hundreds of her Irish sisters in those days, she sought
work in service in the families with houses on Beacon
Hill, in the Back Bay, and in the suburbs of Newton and
Brookline. An immigrant herself, Katie was hired by an
immigrant from eastern Europe, a man who had made it
in the garment business, who had pushed himself out of
the West End of Boston, out of Dorchester, a man who
built a brick house in Chestnut Hill in back of Boston
College. In this house, Katie learned to cook the dishes of
eastern Europe and Russia. People came from two towns

away, from states away to taste Katie's gefilte fish, her matzo balls, her chopped liver, brisket, potato pancakes, her cherry cheesecake. Katie got at least two offers a week from families holding out to her bigger houses, bigger rooms, more pay, more vacation than the typical Thursdays and Sundays, after lunch had been served. Katie helped raise the immigrant's children, and when they were grown, she raised a grandson of the immigrant who was born in the brick house. The grandson was Katie's boy, somehow singled out by her to be Irish, despite his own eastern European forbears. The grandson was educated in the songs and stories of Galway. He could sing "Whiskey You're the Divil" before he could sing "America the Beautiful." Katie used to sit him in his high chair in the middle of the kitchen floor and sing, "My mother sent me out to France to learn the steps of the fogie dance," punctuating it with her own drum solos, spoons on saucepans, and carving knife on crystal glasses.

The radio played the Irish Hour in the kitchen for the grandson, and her friends who worked in the neighborhood came over to gossip about dances at Hibernian Hall in Dorchester, about boat trips to the old country, $5 bills sent home to the family, and deaths of siblings, always deaths. They also celebrated with stories of splendid deeds in life, such as riding in jaunting carts or covering chimneys in one-room schoolhouses with blankets so that school would be let out early because of smoke.

Katie could cure anything—colds, coughs, poison ivy, stomachaches—by laying on of hands and saying the blessing in Gaelic. And every week there were the phone calls for the immigrant grandmother: "Katie, come make chopped liver for us, stuffed derma for us, cheesecake. You want $60 a week? Saint's days off? You tell us." She always resisted. Because it wasn't money that made life bearable. It was loyalty and passion and sense of one's center. No free-agent status for Katie. She was committed to family and committed to love.

Unlike so many modern parents, Katie demanded excellence. Because she gave it, she assumed that it was essential in others. She was profane if you didn't measure up to her standards. The grandson tutored her in her exam for citizenship. "You didn't read it right," she would scold.

"What's for dinner?" The grandson would ask. Superstars didn't give away secrets. "Coobie cootch," Katie would always say . . . cat's feet. Many times she took the grandson to St. Ignatius' Church at Boston College, leaving him to brood in dark silence at the stained glass, the font of holy water. Several times over the years, Archbishop (later Cardinal) Cushing would be there. "Katie," he would scold, "I know he's taken Communion dozens of times. This is a Jewish boy." The Archbishop was always gentle. He knew Katie was the best cook in Boston.

"It doesn't matter, Your Excellency," Katie would insist. "Ask him yourself . . . he's Irish in his heart."

In the summers, the immigrant moved his family to Nantasket beach, south of the city. Next door lived

Bernard Goldfine of Vicuna Coat/Sherman Adams fame, famous during the Eisenhower years. Goldfine was a power broker who threw a medicine ball back and forth in the driveway every morning with his chauffeur. Katie would take the grandson up to her room at night and watch with him out the window into Goldfine's dining room where the governor, Paul Dever, the mayor, Johnny Hynes, the ambassador, Joe Kennedy, another Nantasket boy, often gathered. "Be quiet and listen," Katie would say. "You'll learn what to do when you're a man."

When Katie died recently, she was surrounded by generations of people who loved her, her wake attended by people who sold fabrics in California, maternity fashions in New York, the Quincy High School football team, nurses, builders, real estate developers, secretaries, construction workers, priests, generations of people who knew her wit, her chopped liver, her Toll House cookies, her blessings. The grandson was there. She had bought him the first ever "Superman" magazine, the first "Captain Marvel" issue, and told him, "Sean, save these. They'll be worth a lot of money someday." How many people do you know who are both the best cook in Boston and the best financial advisor? "God is good and Jack is fishin'. . . ."

I am the grandson of that immigrant.

A Life's History

KID MANNING IS THE KIND OF OLD-TIMER YOU feel good about. His eyes are lively. He appreciates women. He can remember both the Czar and Teddy Roosevelt. Kid Manning came to this country in 1893, and he knows Boston at the turn of the century the way you and I know the big Sunday family dinner in current America is going to be either takeout Chinese food or pizza.

Although at age 93, Kid Manning is now old and tired, he has achieved long life with generally excellent health. His attitude about health and longevity has always been an inspiration to me. He is physically a small man, the kind that is always called wiry. His 125 pounds make him only 5 pounds lighter than when he was a professional fighter under the name I am calling him here. Kid Manning is Jewish, but his faith in his body has always been as strong as his faith in Judaism.

Kid Manning has talked to me often about his early days in America. "As a greenhorn kid," he said, " full of wonder, I understood fast that you had to stick up for your rights. You couldn't let yourself be pushed around. That's why my father left Europe. He was a butcher. He could do nothing against the soldiers who would come into our little town, burn houses, stick swords into our beds, into our clothing, looking for money, jewelry, anything of value."

He told me, "The biggest difference between Europe and America, and it amazed me when it first happened, is that in America, when you got in a fight, the other guy always let you up.

"In America, I got into lots of fights. You had to fight because everything was centered on the corner where you'd hang out with your friends. God, my great grandchildren watch television. They have everything, and they complain to me sometimes about having nothing to do. Boredom and self-pity are the two elements that will kill you faster than any disease. You'll be dead between the ears."

Kid Manning spent most of his childhood on the streets, in competition, playing games. He and his friends rolled hoops on the Boston Common, spun tops on the sidewalks, swam in the Charles River, which later became so loaded with bacteria and foreign objects that I had to have a typhoid shot after falling out of a boat into the water in 1960.

"All of our entertainment was outside the home," Kid Manning has told me. "Fruit and vegetable men would peddle their produce from carts outside our window. We would steal ice from the milk cart, and the milkman would chase us through alleys, over fences. He didn't care whether the milk soured or not; the chase after naughty boys was everything. Our year was spent in contests: jumping, running, baseball, swimming, sneaking into burlesque shows. The shows cost 10 cents for the gallery. A dozen of us would come in and individually march by the ticket taker, telling him the next guy would pay for all. The last kid would pay a dime, but by then we would be all over the theater, the show would be starting, and most of us they'd never catch. At the burlesque, it wasn't just stripping. It was variety shows, vaudeville. There I saw gentleman Jim Corbett, who was the light-weight champion. He would do a routine, punch a bag, jump rope, demonstrate his famous solar plexus punch.

"Just about that time a most wonderful thing hap-pened. It was in 1904. They built a gym a few blocks from our house. It changed the life of the gang on the corner because it meant a place to play inside, all winter. And it was also a place to bathe. We all lived in apartment houses. My home was a four-room flat. My mother, my father, and I lived with my three brothers and sisters. There was one bathroom, and we all washed ourselves in the sink. We had a bathtub, but that was where we stored the coal for our stove."

It is marvelously therapeutic to listen to the stories of older people. It is one of the secrets to a satisfying life because it gives you a sense of history that does not come from a book. For years, I have listened to Kid Manning searching for secrets to long life and good health that may go beyond inheritance from the gene pool.

"For my money," he has told me, "there are two things that can ensure a long life with good health. You've got to feel good about yourself. And this means you have to have places of your very own to escape into. I was lucky," he said. "I had two places, sports and music. Sports were easy. We all played everything there was to play. I was a catcher, the leader. Our team was the Hemlocks, from the West End, and we played every town or regional team around Boston. I boxed professional also, at 130 pounds, on barges in the Charles River and in clubs in Cambridge, Boston, and Providence, Rhode Island. That's what the gym taught me. For $15 a fight, I'd go up against all the tough little guys who grew up just like me, whether they were Jewish, Italian, or Irish.

"And you've got to remember," Kid Manning told me, "this was always in our spare time, when we weren't working. All the kids worked; I was a delivery boy for the butcher, a paper boy, I carried ice, I was an usher. Six days a week, after school, and on Saturdays. Did we bitch and moan about it? It was life; everybody in the same boat. When I was getting married, my wife made me stop fighting. It was marriage or boxing. I got married. But I never gave up the love of sports. Two years after our wedding, in 1912 it was, I was going to the store to buy some milk and bread on a Sunday morning. I was wearing a suit and tie and hat like all the other Sunday strollers. At the corner there were all sorts of people gathered. As it happened, that was the starting line for a 15-mile race, a walking race. Walking was a big event then, the shuffling, fast, heel-and-toe event you see in the Olympics. Several of my friends were in the race, in running clothes, including Slobodkin, the harmonica player whom I could beat with one leg. I couldn't help it. I had told my wife I would be right back. But I left my bundle in the bakery, left my hat and tie and jacket also, and entered the race. It was 15 miles up Commonwealth Avenue and back to the starting point. In my street shoes, out of 70 participants, I finished 3rd. I did show up at home with the milk at 7 at night. I still have the cup—pewter, with my name on it.

"The music went along with this," Kid Manning said, "ever since I stood in line for Caruso in 1913 in *The Girl of the Golden West* at the old Boston Theater on Washington Street. I squeezed into standing room in the orchestra. Caruso brought down the house; they wouldn't let him off the stage. He sang an encore, 'The Last Rose of Summer,' and the way the people reacted would make The Beatles look like pishers. That's when I began taking singing lessons and performing in minstrel shows at the West End House, the famous neighborhood settlement house. I always sang a solo, and it was always, 'My Little Gray Home in the West.'"

"You've told me about your secret places," I said to Kid Manning. "What's the other factor that has contributed to your long life?"

Manning smiled. "People nowadays may think it strange," he said, "but I had a hero from the time I was 14. I modeled my life after that hero, tried to emulate him in every respect. The hero was Frank Merriwell, from the dime-novel series. Frank Merriwell played every sport, saved every game. He went from school success to a brilliant career at Yale in about 50 books. Some people who reach old age say they always smoked; others that they chased women or took the occasional cocktail. Frank

Merriwell never smoked or drank," said Kid Manning. "And he invariably triumphed in every sport and in life. I followed his life then, I follow him now. I went to every Harvard–Yale game from 1905 through 1970 and yelled like hell for Yale. My oldest boy went to Yale, my other sons to Penn, where they played baseball and ran the hurdles. I'll be 94 years old in a few weeks, but I've never found any reason to have a better hero than Frank Merriwell."

Kid Manning used to play catch with me until he was in his late 80s. He had a battered catcher's mitt from the 1920s that he would take every spring to the Boston Braves Florida training camp, where he'd pester the players to throw to him. After the Braves left for Milwaukee, he would take his glove and follow the Red Sox to Sarasota. The "Goddam Red Sox," he called them. He always threw a heavy ball and always aimed to hit me in the chest with his throw. The last time we played, he could still throw a bigger curve than I could ever manage in my life. And I was a lefty, where the curve should have been natural.

I visited Kid Manning recently in the hospital. He is finally winding down, his frame shrunken, his body fighting more problems than a dress manufacturer in bankruptcy. He is worn out, but is still glad to see me. His handshake is dry and firm. His hands are large for the rest of him, the hands of a catcher, of a fighter. He feels as if his lessons have to be re-emphasized while he has time.

"Exercise your body," he tells me. "Break away from where you spend your days. And always have a place for the soul to escape to. Listen to people if you want them to care about you. Have a hero. It sometimes allows you to believe in yourself more, and to keep up the fight." Kid Manning lies back on his pillow. He is exhausted, and it is time for me to leave. As I head for the door, he calls to me and holds up his right hand. He flashes one finger at me, then two.

"What's that?" I ask him.

"Remember," he says to me, "one finger for a fast ball, two for a curve."

Kid Manning is my grandfather.

Every family is its own soap opera, and you all know you cannot make up the things that are true in life. For the holidays this year, one of the things I gave to my children was a framed photograph of my grandfather dressed as Pagliacci, starring in a production of the opera in 1908. He was a tenor. One of my kids sings in a heavy metal band. A long way from Pagliacci. But he was thrilled to look at his great grandfather, singing in costume, thrilled at the continuity, and the history.

And what you can learn from this family story is that always, in good times and bad, your emotions and attitudes will play a dominant factor in your success or failure. Daily, in the volatile trading that will be with us for years to come, the markets are going to be buffeted by rumor and news and collective frenzies that mostly have nothing to do with rational thought. And your best chance to survive the uncertainties and absurdities will be in your ability to find your own special places, perhaps reach into the past and escape from the challenges of the daily world, and your willingness to live up to the standards set by the heroes you choose for yourself.

The Dinosaur Club

E VERY COLLEGE STUDENT IN THE 1950s AND 1960s at some point in his or her academic career had to study Margaret Mead and her research (among other things) on tribes and tribal behavior. But all tribes change and evolve. The same is true in business; we must change or die. Anyone old enough to have had an actual house call from a doctor knows how much the practice of medicine has changed.

I had dinner last week with three men who call themselves the Dinosaur Club. They are all in their late 50s, and they all work the institutional side of the investment business. This means that they buy or sell stocks and bonds to and from professional investors like banks, insurance companies, and mutual funds. The three men are Peter Caruso, who runs a bond trading desk, T. J. Faherty, who heads equity trading for one of the largest brokers, and Mel Wheelock, an equity salesman, who mainly sells his firm's research ideas to fund managers. They are talking about the fight to hang on in a business they are afraid has passed them by.

"We had street smarts," Faherty said. "We started at $5,000 a year and were told to keep our eyes and ears open. Now the trading desks only hire brilliant kids from the Ivy League at 80 grand. And they don't want to look at anyone from commuter colleges. We'd never get jobs in our firms if we were interviewing today." They each ordered single malt scotch. Peter Caruso asked the waiter to "put one ice cube in my glass, swirl it around, and pour it out. Then put in the scotch." He smiled at us. "That's what I learned from my Protestant friends," he said. "Years ago when they owned most of the firms. As for the other firms, the German Jews were worse snobs than the Protestants."

"Well, I said we'd never be hired today," Faherty went on. "But my son's at Yale, majoring in economics. So which is the worse condition, and which is better?"

"There used to be such loyalty in the business," Wheelock said. "We all protected each other. I remember when guys would be so hung over from the night before, they'd go right to the Turkish baths in the morning and never show up for work. But everyone on the street covered for you; orders would come in for your credit; your boss always took care of you. Today, they step over your body."

"Lunches were the thing," Faherty added. "Business was done over lunch."

"I remember my first week as a wet-behind-the-ears kid," Wheelock said. "My boss took me out to Brandy Joe's, the gin mill where you'd walk in and Joe would greet you at the door and say, 'This guy'll never last. . . . Buy me a brandy because I'll probably never see you again.' And you had to buy him a brandy. Then you'd have a see-through (a martini) or two with the boys, and we'd talk shop and sports, and then some fund manager would come by to meet the new kid. He'd shake my hand, welcome me to the biz, and stick a piece of paper in my breast pocket. Then he'd wish me luck and walk away. I'd pull the slip of paper out, open it, and it would say, 'Buy 50,000 Arco at the market.' A 50,000 share order on Atlantic Richfield. My first week. That's how they used to do it."

When you read about or hear people talk about the "sell" side in the investment business, it means brokerage firms that try to sell stock and bond ideas to institutions like banks and mutual funds, to pension funds and insurance companies. The "buy" side of the business is represented by these institutions that buy the ideas in the form of stocks and bonds, and other products like derivatives. The three men in the Dinosaur Club are all from the sell side. They are salesmen. "Entertainment was our business," T. J. Faherty went on. "I once said to the president of our firm, 'I can save you a million dollars a year.'"

"'How can you do that, T. J.?' he said."

"'You spend a million a year on research,'" I told him, "'on analysts' reports. I say that you forget about analysts' research reports with dozens of pages. Fire them all and staple together four blank pages. In the middle put in six tickets to the Knicks and the Celtics. That's all the research you need.'"

"Of course," Wheelock added, "that's how the business was done. Relationships. I remember when I got a job for one of my drinking buddies, Johnny Muldoon, who was at Kidder Peabody. He was a trader, and he wanted to move to the buy side, and he interviewed with Mr. Gardner III, chairman of one of the biggest mutual funds in town. Of course, Mr. Gardner's first question to Johnny was, 'Where did you attend college?' This was key for Mr. Gardner III. Johnny looked at him and said, 'I went to Nonè University.' Mr. Gardner smiled and nodded, figuring it was some Jesuit school he never heard of. Later, he found out that it was *none*; Muldoon never got past high school. Then Gardner III laughed like hell."

"The people who ran the firms years ago understood. They got it. And they protected their people. Sandy Weill, in his old Shearson days, knew every single employee. And most of their wives' names, too. You think they wouldn't kill for him?" Peter Caruso ordered us more single malt. "We used to do this at lunch," he said. "That's where the business was done. Lunch. Sometimes the lunches would spill into dinner. And years ago, some ladies of the night would show up in our private dining rooms. One night one of the old-time waiters came into the room; Sal was his name. 'Mr. Caruso,' he said, 'What do you think? I would swap the tip for a participation.' He was very formal about it."

"That's the night you got stopped by the cop," Wheelock remembered.

"I was already stopped," Caruso said. "I pulled over next to a fire alarm, thinking the globe above it was a red traffic light. The cop says, 'Sir, can I see your driver's license?' So I handed him my American Express card, and he said, 'We don't take those, sir.'"

"Drinking and driving," Wheelock said, "that's one of the biggest changes in the game. That's all over, thank God."

"It's all over," Faherty added. "Remember our annual St. Paddy's Day adventure? Some 20 to 30 of us, buy side and sell side, we'd go to watch the parade, and have a giant do at Callahans. One year, we thought we needed to cool off, go have a dip at the Y opposite Callahans. Eight or ten of us went in, all half in the bag, and it's 'old ladies afternoon,' any woman over 50. Well, there are 15 or 20 of them, shrieking, yelling, laughing. So what do we do? Off with the clothes, jump in the pool with the ladies. We're all laughing ourselves sick, pinching and giggling, the girls and the boys. Best St. Paddy's Day I ever had, and if I remember correctly, a shitload of stock changed hands that week, for all the guys who were in the pool."

The Dinosaurs sipped their single malt. Faherty raised his glass to the others, "Confusion to our enemies," he said. The others repeated the toast.

"I used to think I could work in this business till I dropped," Wheelock said. "I loved the market, I loved the people. I couldn't imagine retiring if you adore where you show up during the day. Last week, though, some young blood in New York, on the trading desk, tells me I'm 'out of the loop.' Can you imagine some wise-ass telling me I'm out of the loop? For years, I held the city's record for shares traded in one day. Out of the loop. . . ."

"You know," Caruso said, "the big difference today is selfishness. The firms are loyal to no one. And the workers are only loyal to themselves as well. The young couples today all work, but unlike us, they have a plan. The plan is to bust their ass together and have enough dough to walk away at 40. Hasta luego! We never had a plan."

"But the poor bastards," Faherty said, "will never remember when it was fun; when it was life."

The Dinosaur Club know their priorities; they've had their fun. But make sure you stop to think about what you're getting from the way you're handling your money, and make sure you know what your goals are. Do you just want to make money? Or are you looking for a life?

Living by Accident

I SEE DOZENS OF YOUNG PEOPLE EACH YEAR, coming out of college and high school, nervous about their future and what's going to happen to them. Up to those graduation points, almost everything has been planned for them by parents and their schools. I tell them all, "Don't worry about your future. Life is going to happen to you no matter how much you worry about it." A corollary to this is: Nothing is probably going to happen the way you plan it. It may work out much better than you planned. But it most likely never will be what you planned. Along with this advice, which I know is right, is the accidental nature of things. I tell those young people seeking counsel, "Who cares that you have no idea what you want to do after college? Most people who are truly interesting have no idea what their career paths will be. I feel sorry for kids who know at age 11 that they want to be doctors and lawyers. It's going to limit their education and experience."

Most young people feel better about their own situation hearing this. Then I tell them, "Ask any three adults if they had any idea in their early 20s where their careers might take them." I am always surprised when anyone could predict his or her own path.

Before any young person leaves a career session with me, I also say, "And if you ever choose to marry, this above all else is probably a cosmic accident: who walks into a room at the right time or the wrong time. Don't worry too much about it." Occasionally, I tell them how my wife and I got together, a series of accidents and misadventures, but somehow typical of these things. And you can count the ironies along the way.

I was a senior in college, dating in a nonserious way. One spring weekend, my current girlfriend suggested a picnic for Saturday, at a beach on the north shore of our city. She wanted to fix up two of her friends and proposed that I find two appropriate guys. I asked two of my best friends, classmates who had performed with me in a satirical musical that year and certainly knew how to picnic. But the two friends were very competitive, and I didn't want the outing spoiled by their squabbling over who got which date. I knew that one of the blind dates was blond and one brunette. So I made the boys flip a coin; heads won the blond, tails the brunette, no arguments, no second-guessing. My friend David won the brunette, Barbara, and because we all believe in fairy tales, don't we? They fell in love on their first date.

I have a picture of them on this outing, David playing his guitar and singing to Barbara, the old English folk song, "Blow the Candles Out." They were married a year later, and because of his job, moved around the globe, six locations in seven years. Every time they'd come back to visit Barbara's parents, I'd go over for a visit, and every time they'd come to town, there was Barbara's baby sister, Susan, at home as well. But Susan had done a lot of growing up since her brunette sister had dated and married. She was modeling in Boston, looking increasingly splendid, every time I dropped in. There is a time to be sneaky in life. I couldn't just ask her out; I had known the family too long. I was seven years older than Susan, and her family already called me a dirty old man (in my mid-20s). They would have been horrified if I asked her out. So I said, "Susan, I've got endless friends you'd love. I'd be thrilled to fix you up with some great guys." Indeed, I arranged a date for the next Saturday night with Parker, one of my best in-town buddies. "But," I told Susan, "how about we have dinner Thursday night so I can actually get an idea of what you're like. So I can fix you up with people who would really be compatible."

She bought that, and we had dinner Thursday night. On Friday morning, I called Parker and said, "I've got good news for you and bad news."

"What's the good news?" Parker asked.

"I've met this wonderful woman," I told him. "I'm in love for the first time in my life."

"That's great," Parker said. "What's the bad news?"

"You don't have a date Saturday night."

And we got married about a year later, her family resigned to the fact that perhaps even dirty old men had their soft spots.

There are endless ironies in how people meet and mate, and what jobs they take, and where they set down roots. But young people anxious about their own lives and careers should not worry needlessly about what will happen to them. Often, it's something as simple as a coin flip that determines where we go. Cosmic accidents.

Along these lines, it's wise to understand that accidents play great parts in the major events of history, both political and economic. And that headline news often grows from very simple beginnings. Sanford Weill of Travelers and John Reed of Citibank are forging the largest financial services merger in history, Citigroup, an $83 billion combination that would dwarf any other institution of its kind in the world.

Sandy Weill, then the chairman of Travelers, tells the story of the merger proposal in a way that puts these great events in perspective—just as the smart investor must always put such events under a commonsense telescope so as to relate them to a simple understanding. "The more I thought about the potential combination," Weill has said, "the more I thought it was a great idea. So I called John Reed and told him that I had an exciting idea proposal for him. We were both going to be in Washington at the same time in the next week or so, and I suggested breakfast or lunch or whatever fit his schedule."

Weill has a delightfully self-effacing, modest delivery that, after forty odd years of business success, still reflects an enormous sense of wonder and inspires fierce loyalty from his troops. "Reed couldn't do breakfast or lunch," Weill went on, "but he could see me after dinner and came up to my room a little after ten." He paused and smiled, "I'm not sure how I felt about having a man in my bedroom after ten." Then he said, "I gave Reed my merger proposal, and there was silence. Then Reed laughed and said, "This is unbelievable. You are initiating the biggest merger in history. And I thought all this time you were going to ask me to take a table at a charity benefit."

Absurdities in life do surface at every turn. One of the smartest things I ever heard from a lawyer was from a street smart woman client who recently became a judge. After years of doing domestic legal work, she told me, "Divorce most often comes down to the fight over the pink plastic vase in the bathroom." It will help you all in your investments and in your lives to keep the right perspective on what seems at the time to be overwhelming.

When it comes to the most important decisions in your life, make the best choices you can, but be prepared to turn the surprises life hands you to your advantage. Don't be shocked if some of your biggest opportunities seem to happen by chance. Not needing to know what comes next is a key part of living an interesting, productive, and successful life.

Family Dramas and
the Markets

IF YOU FIND THE STUDY OF HISTORY BORING,
then look into the history of your own families, or
the families of your friends. As you come to know them
better—with their follies and their triumphs—you'll come
to know yourself better. And the better you understand
the absurdities of life, the better you will understand some
of the less tangible factors that can change the course of
the markets—as well as your own investments.

What exactly can you learn about money and the
stock market from your family? For starters, that not
everything will go according to plan.

A friend of mine, a lawyer with a philosophical
bent, has two sons. During their teenage years, the older
son, David, was obsessed with the group The Grateful
Dead. He followed them everywhere, referred to them
constantly, tried to mimic their lifestyle. "I called David
and all his friends," the lawyer told me, "The Ungrateful
Living." His wife and he despaired of David ever wearing
decent clothes, of ever going to college, or ever having a
job. The younger son went away for high school to a
fancy boarding school where he attended chapel, got
straight As, wore a tie and jacket at all times, and listened
to Broadway tunes and Bach.

"Wonder of wonders," my friend said to me, "years
go by and David, my oldest son, is working at a bank,

ground floor, marble and mahogany, part of a young blood hit team, loaning big bucks to rich people all over the world. This is the kid who swore he'd never wear a tie ever in his life. Now he looks like he's Ralph Lauren's son, for God's sake, not mine. And all he talks about is the place of the banker in society, and whether it's prudent to loan someone money to buy a set of Purdey shotguns made in 1921. One day last week, David's on two lines, pinning down a customer, and the younger brother, Kenny, the formerly buttoned-down kid, now in college, careens onto David's marble floor at work, riding a skateboard. His hair is shoulder length, he's got a hoop earring in his left ear, and he's wearing a jean jacket to which he's attached 1,000 safety pins as decoration. Two security guards chase him across the floor to David's desk. The two brothers get in a shouting contest until cooler heads prevail. You never know," my friend added.

Part of what you can learn from family stories like this one is that life is not pure. So much that happens to us is an accident, and whatever we plan for probably is not going to turn out as we planned. It may be much better, not worse. But it will undoubtedly not be as we had imagined. The markets are not rational—and the stocks you hold do not know that you own them. Don't hold out for "sure things" in your investments—these are surely illusory. Successful investing, like successful parenting, depends on your making the best choices you can—and learning to accept the uncertainty of the results.

The Least Likely to Succeed

IT HAS COST ALL OF US PROBABLY A LOT OF money over the years because of a childhood bias that most of us share. Remember Little Stinky from the playground in the third grade? The fat kid everyone teased or the adolescent everyone called Specks because of his acne? Cruel, of course, because in many ways, childhood is the cruelest time of all. These two unfortunate kids are apocryphal. But we all know the "Stinkys" who grew up to be fabulously wealthy or the "Specks" who became a Hollywood star. And we never would have believed it. Because we all remember the schoolyard, and can never believe that people we actually knew and went to school with could make it big in life. And particularly—make it bigger than us.

A friend of mine tells me that he lives in a small neighborhood. But within a block of his house live three billionaires, all at one time (or currently) CEOs of companies widely known in America. He asked various neighbors if they owned stock in those companies. Invariably, everyone he asked said, "No." And there were various reasons: "I see him in jogging clothes"; "I heard he was very stern with his children"; "I knew he was kind of a mediocre student in college."

The truth is, because we have actually known a CEO, or a celebrity, or a billionaire, we somehow say, "Hey, they put their pants on one leg at a time. Same as me. Therefore, they must be like me, and it's luck they got to where they are. Or maybe they inherited it. If he hadn't gotten a stake from his father-in-law . . . ."

My rule of thumb now is to remember that Little Stinky and Specks desperately wanted revenge for the humiliations of their youth and that their hunger to win drove them to success. Never bet on the most likely to succeed from your schooldays. In most cases, that was his or her finest hour. But be prepared to bet on, and ride with, the people who bear the scars from their past, who are driven to prove something.

So Smart, They're Stupid

AMONG MY FATHER'S MANY ACCOMPLISHMENTS was to have read the *Encyclopedia Britannica* (1950 edition) from beginning to end, from Aachen through Zyzzyvd. It took him years, but he did it.

For someone who prized learning as much as he did, he was contemptuous of lots of academics. "He's so smart, he's stupid," he would often say to me about someone of his acquaintance who had great book knowledge but very little ability to adapt it to the practical world.

Along those same lines, I have known many men who have run very successful companies but have been absolute disasters in managing their own private funds. "What the hell is wrong with the stock market?" these people would invariably complain to me. "Every time I zig, it zags. And vice versa. You want to make money in the market, do the opposite of everything I do." You'd be amazed at how many so-called smart people say exactly the same thing.

One of my smartest clients, a man who runs a billion-dollar conglomerate that does everything from tire retailing to movie production, called me after the market had plunged almost 2,000 points in the fall of 1998. "First of all," he said, "it's my money, don't talk me out of anything. Second of all, I travel all around the world, and the world is going to hell. I want out of everything. Cash will be king."

"But you're not selling your businesses, are you?"

"Are you nuts? Why would I do that?"

He had confidence in his abilities to prosper in *any* business climate. During the Great Depression of the 1930s, my father's family was wiped out. My mother's family had a cook and a chauffeur, and slid through the bad times. Why? My maternal grandfather made maternity underwear—and he had key customers who kept him producing all through those depressed times: luck, a hot product, customers who wanted to feed him business, a combination of all three.

Remember that the same concept applies to the stock market, and my smart client should have known this. Even in a Depression, there are companies that thrive, stocks that can do well. When suffering is rampant, not everyone suffers. Running his own company, my client is smart. Reacting to his personal investments, he is emotional and often stupid.

A classic example of this: After the average New York Stock Exchange stock had declined 40 percent in the summer and fall of 1998, and the average NASDAQ stock fell over 50 percent from the highs, a client who is a management consultant called and demanded that I liquidate all of his holdings. Over three years, I had produced annual gains for this conservative consultant of over 20 percent, which certainly beats a sharp stick in the eye.

"Do you want to hear my speech first?" I asked.

"I don't want to hear your speech," the consultant answered. "Do I have to remind you that I am a PhD from MIT?"

"It's you people who got us in all this trouble," I answered, thinking of the Nobel Prize winners who helped take the hedge fund Long-Term Capital almost down the drain.

Having a high IQ is no guarantee of success in the stock market. Beware of people who are so smart, they're stupid. And if you're in danger of being one of these people, listen to your stomach as well as your brain when you're making key investment decisions.

A Little Something
on the Side

A COLLEGE CLASSMATE, POLITE TO A FAULT, called me after our 20th college reunion. "I think I'm going to give you our money to watch," he said. "But you were way too racy in college, and I want to make sure you know I'm conservative, conservative, conservative. Get it? Nothing racy!"

"I get it," I told him. "Conservative."

Two years after he had become a client, I was going over one of his monthly brokerage statements and saw that he had written a check for $10,000 to some penny stock promoter's firm in Salt Lake City, Utah. A firm the SEC was trying to shut down. I couldn't believe it.

"What the hell are you doing in Salt Lake City?" I asked, speaking to him as if he were a philandering husband and had strayed from his wife. After some coaxing, he admitted, "I got several calls that intrigued me, about titanium, a strategic metal. We use it for defense, and they told me it's in short supply (the cold war was still on), and South Africa and the Middle East are going to explode—and so is the price of titanium. They've got a mine loaded with it. In Nevada."

"What happened to conservative?" I asked him. "You're doing great with your GE, your Merck. Weren't you going to tell me about this, sneaking the ten grand out of the account to some sleazeball?" Silence on the other end. Then . . . "It's $20,000 now, I'm afraid," he said. "It's an extraordinary opportunity."

"You're going to lose it all," I told him. "It's the oldest scam in the book."

"Look," my classmate said, "GE and Merck are fine. And, I suppose, I admit you're fine. But you and those stocks are like my wife. I'm old-fashioned in lots of ways. Salt Lake City and titanium are like my mistress. Give a guy a little life, will you?"

Of course, he lost the $20,000 and was too ashamed of going after the cold callers. He even told me, "Don't send any annual reports or quarterlies on the titanium company to my house. I don't want my wife to see." Some people's pornography is someone else's titanium. And everyone deserves a little raciness, even in their portfolios.

Surprise!

IT'S THE LAST DAY OF THE YEAR. I'M SITTING IN MY office looking out over the Boston Common and, in the distance, Fenway Park. Out of the windows on the other side of the office I can see the lights on Boston Harbor, the airport, and the harbor islands beyond.

I like to be in the office alone, late in the afternoon at the end of the year, to reflect on things that have happened in the past and on what may occur in the year to come. My crew and I shared some champagne before they all left for the evening. I'm having the last of it in a plastic cup.

During the day, a young man came into my office. He works for us and is a relative rookie, having come into the financial business in the last two years. Danny is smart and hard working but seemed ironically sad as he came in to wish me a happy New Year.

"Everything's moving so fast," he said. "How the hell am I going to make it in this business? My wife just got a job offer in San Francisco, my in-laws live in Dallas, my folks are now in Florida, my sisters and brothers live all over the place, and the ones that are married don't seem to have any roots, or connections, to anything. Other than e-mail and their computers.

"It's a brave new world out there," I said.

"You're telling me," Danny answered. "And I think it's frightening. Where is everyone's center?"

"You're a little young to be so philosophical. That's my job."

He smiled. "It just seems we all are going to be lost in cyberspace," he said. "In 50 years, no one will have any arms or legs. We'll just move that mouse with our nose; no human contact. "

"You're just suffering year end syndrome," I told Danny. "Lack of melatonin. You need some sunshine, that's all. As for this business, and any other service profession for that matter, people need common sense, advice, and counsel more than they ever have—because of the society we're in today, which is increasingly anonymous. If you offer this personal advice and counsel, you'll be as busy as you want to be. This is what the world needs, someone to hold out their hand, and be a guide."

He held his palm open, waiting for me to slap it— one of the rituals of daily life. "I still see this cartoon on your door," Danny said.... 'Shudda, cudda, wudda... Next!'"

"It's the American way," I said.

All during this last day of the year, people called with last-minute crises: opening Roth IRAs, channeling out retirement distributions, executing tax strategies, dispensing funds for charitable giving—all intensely personal, all hoping to give some measure of what we all long for . . . peace of mind.

I am big on surprises. I was wearing an unusual present that I had received a week before. Hanging from our front doorknob as I put out the trash late one night was a velvet bag. In the bag was a gift-wrapped box. And a note. "I recall," it said, "there is an ancient Chinese tradition that urges one to give to the complimentor that which was complimented. Whether that is the case or not, I decided the evening I took these off that it was time for them to begin a new life! To me they came from a dear friend who has vanished though not from my memory: So from me they should go to another dear friend who is still very much around and who will show them a good time. Yes, there still is a Santa Claus!"

In the box were an exquisite pair of enamel-and-gold cufflinks, circles the size of quarters in red and yellow and green, looking as if they could have belonged to Cary Grant or Douglas Fairbanks, Jr. in the days when men knew how to dress. The present bowled me over— and reinforced my belief in the importance of surprise. Having a sense of wonder is a strong element in the truly admirable life.

My office was dark except for one small lamp that I had turned on at the end of a couch. I sipped my champagne in the silence, looking out upon the brightness of the city at holiday time. A knock on my office door surprised me. "I took the chance you might be in," a man's voice said. "You like to sit in the dark?" When the man came in, I saw it was someone whom I had known for years, someone with whom I had never done business.

The man, I know, had retired from running one of the largest insurance firms in the world.

"I was seeing my lawyer," he told me, "and, as you know, there is a certain rhythm to life; you've been on my mind, and well, here I am."

We both looked out at the city, lit up and seeming to hold out all sorts of promise, as New Year's Eve tends to do.

"Well," I finally said. "Do you want to make money—or would you rather fool around?"

He reached into a shopping bag and pulled out a bottle of wine, with a red ribbon tied around the neck. He put the bottle on my desk.

"It's about time I made some money in the market," he said.

"Fine with me," I answered. "It's never too late to make money." I picked up the bottle. "And I have a corkscrew," I added. "Good to keep a corkscrew in the office. . . . You never know."

Boston, Massachusetts

Index